Minus One

A story of loss, grieving, acceptance, healing...
and finding love again

Gregg Bonn

Same Publishing, Scottsdale AZ

ISBN 979-8-9863372-1-0 (Paperback edition)

ISBN 979-8-9863372-0-3 (Hardcover edition)

ISBN 979-8-9863372-2-7 (Ebook edition)

Contents

Part Three
Takeaways

Note from the Author

The majority of dated entries in this book are excerpted from Facebook posts, which I began using in earnest on August 31, 2015. Prior to my delving into Facebook with these posts, I had rarely used my account. This was a new venture for me, and what began as the only way I knew to contact those who loved Heidi evolved into a way for me to process and heal from my grief. Some posts have been edited slightly. Narrative segments follow posts to flesh out the story.

Part One

The End and The Beginning

Prologue

I was waiting in the hall outside the hospital room where Heidi was being treated for complications of an aggressive form of cancer, when the doctor came out and told me, "It's going to be soon."

"What do you mean, soon?" I asked him, "I have three kids in school."

"I suggest you go get them." He looked serious.

"Her brother is flying in later today. Can't you stall?" I don't know what I was thinking. I wasn't thinking.

A nurse exited Heidi's room and pulled the doctor in. Within minutes he returned.

"Forget getting the kids," he said. "It's happening now."

Chapter 1

Gone

August 31, 2015, 3:18 p.m.

Today, I lost the love of my life.
    Rest in peace Heidi.
    You will be missed.

August 31, 2015, 3:25 p.m.

I am devastated to announce the passing of Heidi.
    Today she lost her battle with cancer.
    She leaves behind a massive void of goodness.
    The world will be so much less without her.

August 31, 2015 changed my life forever. The last eighteen years of my life lay before me, taking her last breath. Holding her hand, I saw her chest rise for the very last time. In a moment, it was over. The nurse noted the time—10:04 a.m. Our fight was done. I stood motionless over her lifeless body in disbelief, gently rubbing my fingers through her short hair, remembering how long and beautiful it had always been. I could feel every strand, soft against my fingertips. I bent over and kissed my wife for the very last time; then I left the room, taking my first steps into a new life.

Just outside her room, and a lifetime away, I began to make a few necessary phone calls as best I could. I called my parents and then Nancy, one of Heidi's closest friends. I had spoken to Nancy less than an hour before while following the ambulance to the hospital. I told her I would contact her when we were checked in, and she could come see Heidi then. I called back sooner than she expected with something different to say.

"Heidi is gone," I explained. She didn't understand. She asked what I meant by "gone."

"Heidi just passed away," I reiterated.

Upon hearing this news, she remained calm to support me; she would be the strength I didn't have.

I asked her to go get the kids, and she said, "No, I will come get you and we will get them together."

For the kids, today had started just like any other day. They woke up, had breakfast, got ready, and went to school. Before their departure, Madeline and Jack told their mother goodbye and that they loved her; Heidi reciprocated. When Max left forty-five minutes later, he came into the bedroom, hugged his mom, told her he loved her and said goodbye. It didn't occur to any of them that they had just said goodbye to their mother for the very last time.

The task of telling my kids their mother had died stood before me like an unsurpassable mountain range. How would I deliver this message to them? How would I break their hearts as mine had been broken? Nancy was on her way to the hospital and would drive me to the kids' schools and help me with this horrific task. I was grateful.

I struggled with having to be the one to tell my children. Maybe I could tell them that Mom was in the hospital and really sick and they needed to come and see her. Then I could let the social workers, who are trained to do this, tell them. No sooner had the thought occurred to me than I realized I wouldn't be able to pull that off. I wouldn't be able to hide the reality on my face, and I wouldn't be able to lie to my kids. The only way was forward. This task was mine and mine alone. It had to be me.

Nancy arrived in the emergency room lobby. She walked through the automatic doors and looked at me; her expression spoke for her. As we embraced, I was comforted by another who shared my deep love for Heidi. Nancy and I would be forever connected by this moment. We walked back to the room where Heidi lay peacefully, so Nancy could see her friend one last time and say goodbye. But time kept moving; we had to leave and get the kids.

We arrived at the middle school where Madeline and Jack were going about their day, oblivious to the news they were about to receive that would change them forever, too. I had no idea what the protocol was for something of this magnitude. Should counselors be present when they were told? I'd never before had to tell my children their mother died. This was uncharted territory. The pain was still so fresh it was difficult to tell the front-desk receptionist why I was there, but I managed to mumble through my tears what had happened and that I needed to pull the children out of school. By the look on her face it was clear that she, too, was not ready to receive such news. She got on her hand-held radio, and within minutes the assistant principal and guidance counselor were standing in front of me. They would take Madeline and Jack out of class and bring them to an office where I could be with them in private.

Jack told me later, "The teacher said I needed to go to the office. I asked her if I should bring my stuff. She said yes. As I walked to the office, something felt wrong. It felt as though something had happened, something with Mom. They wouldn't just call me to the office with my stuff if it wasn't serious." The thought that his mother had died began to haunt him as he completed each step. He tried to convince himself that he was wrong and maybe it was something else, but he knew; he just had that feeling.

Madeline's experience was similar. The assistant principal walked into her art class. "I noticed him and thought nothing of it; what were the odds that he was there to speak to me? He approached me and complimented me on the drawing I was working on. He told me to grab my things and come with him to the office. I immediately began to think about Mom." Madeline's heart began to beat faster, and her legs began to weaken as she approached the office. She didn't know what was going on, and she had no idea what was about to happen. "I first saw Jack there, and then when I saw Dad come in, I knew this wasn't good."

Soon I was summoned to see my children. Thoughts of what to say and how to act ran through my head. I wanted to show strength, but I had none. I wanted to say the right thing, but I had no words. There was no preparation for what I had to do. I forced my legs to move down the hall and get closer to the office that was hiding my kids. My heart was pounding, and my breathing was labored. I had to calm myself. I entered. There they were, with surprised looks on their faces. They weren't expecting to see me at school that day. I tried to think of a way to soften the news I had to deliver, but when I opened my mouth, this is what came out: "Your mother died this morning."

Once I released those words, my children aged instantly as they stood before me in disbelief. They stared at me in silence as tears began to roll down their faces. I grabbed and hugged them. I held them close and tight as if to reassure them that we were still together, that although broken, we were still a family. I needed to reassure myself of the same thing.

Delivering that news to my two oldest children had been excruciating, but there was still one who didn't know. I had to recompose myself and do the whole thing all over again with my youngest child, Max. Max's school wasn't far from the middle school, just a few blocks, so I didn't have much time to agonize. Upon arrival, I reenacted the routine. I went to the front desk and requested a few moments with the principal. I informed her of what had happened and was escorted to her office, where I could wait to receive Max.

Max described the experience to me. "Over the intercom, I heard, 'Please send Max to the office.' There were two Maxes in the class, so I asked the teacher which one, and she said me. I grabbed my stuff and began to walk to the office. I was extremely confused and didn't know why I was going. I started to get a bad feeling in my stomach that something bad had happened." Once Max saw me his fears were confirmed. When I told him the news, he shattered before me into a million pieces. He had no words; he could only hold me tight so he wouldn't be lifted off the planet into the black hole that had just been created. His tears dampened my shirt; his mother was gone.

The ride to the hospital was a road of tears, unbelievably sad. The kids tried to make sense of what didn't make sense. The boys tried to understand why. Why their mother? She was such a good person. Why couldn't this have happened to a bad person, someone who hurt or killed someone else, someone who deserved it? Why did this have to happen to our family? Madeline tried to find some tiny measure of a positive spin, saying, "At least Mom isn't in pain anymore; at least she's finally free of cancer."

When we arrived at the hospital we were greeted by an on-staff social worker. She was soft-spoken, gentle, and a calming figure in what, for our family, was anything but a calm day. She escorted us through double doors and into the maze of ER treatment rooms. Down several halls and around corners, we arrived at a closed-door waiting room. It was an interior room with no windows; chairs lined the walls, and in the middle was a coffee table hosting a fruit and cookie tray.

This was the death room. This was the room where you were brought to come to terms with what had just happened outside; where you tried to find some comfort in the worst day of your life. This room had seen far too much grief.

After a bit, our social worker asked the kids if they wanted to go see their mother. Such a simple question, yet such a monumental answer. The internal debate played out uniquely for each of the three kids. The decision to go or not to go would have lasting effects. I knew the decision had to be theirs alone.

Jack and Max needed to see Heidi one last time, even at risk of what the last image of their mother would be. Madeline could not go. She couldn't bear for her last memory of her mother to be lying in a hospital bed, lifeless. She wanted to remember the good and happy times, not the bad cancer times. She felt that if she went to that room, she wouldn't be able to unsee what she saw.

The boys and I walked through the maze to Heidi's room. Madeline remained behind with Nancy. Judy, Heidi's mom, was there, still by Heidi's side. Heidi's coloring was a tinted yellow from jaundice. She lay on the bed restfully, as if taking a nap. She wore the clothing she'd arrived in and looked at peace. This was the image my boys walked in to. They approached her bed and stood there, silent. I felt as if I could hear the sounds of their hearts breaking. Max was ten and Jack, barely twelve —too young to be standing there seeing what they saw. One at a time, they approached their mother, bent over, hugged her, kissed her, and then left the room.

Soon after, it was time for Judy and me to leave, too. The permanence of walking out that door haunted me. I felt rooted to the ground, unable to take a step. Eight months before, when Heidi had been diagnosed, Judy and I had promised her we would never leave her by herself. We promised to fight this battle alongside her and support her in any way we could. Our commitment was unconditional. Now, released from our vow, we were lost. We could no longer help her; we could no longer stay by her side. We had to leave her, and as we walked out that door into the hall, for the first time, Heidi was truly alone.

Chapter 2

The "C" Word

I was not prepared to lose Heidi so quickly. Her death came at me rapidly and without warning. As a true believer in Heidi's unbreakable spirit and unparalleled determination, I'd had every reason to believe she would beat cancer.

The cancer had arrived only eight months before, with a quick phone call from the oncologist's office. Heidi was breathless and could not pick it up. I grabbed the handset and walked out of the room.

"Gregg, this is Dr. Jamison. It's cancer." She paused. "Heidi has small cell carcinoma, and it's very aggressive. We need to start treatment right away."

I walked back into the room and put the doctor on speakerphone so Heidi could listen. The doctor repeated what she had said and went on to detail the sense of urgency to begin the treatments. Heidi would start chemo in the hospital the next day.

After we hung up the phone, we said nothing. Heidi was sitting on the bed, and I was standing before her. Heidi's head fell into my chest, and we hugged each other and cried.

If Heidi had researched her cancer, she would have discovered that small cell carcinoma, when diagnosed at stage four, carries a two percent survival rate, with most patients dying within four to six months after diagnosis. Once she had learned this, she would not have been able to forget it; she would have been completely demoralized. Heidi chose not to research it, preferring instead to choose hope. I would follow her lead and do the same.

We couldn't remain in despair for long, because we had to tell the kids. After several minutes we began to compose ourselves. I don't know where Heidi found the strength, but she drew it from some place deep. Normally, I am the one to deliver bad news, like when we told the kids we'd lost our house and had to move. That night, however, I had no voice.

The kids joined us in the master bedroom, and we all found a spot on the bed. Heidi looked at each of them and said, "I have cancer, but don't worry. I'm going to do whatever it takes to make sure that I beat this thing so I can stay with you guys and see you grow up. You're the most important part of my life."

She said it all without crying. She said it without a shift in her breathing. It was very matter-of-fact, strong and confident. The resolve that came through was intense, and we all knew that what she was saying was truth. It was a foregone conclusion that this cancer was just going to be a little hiccup in our lives, and I know it was Heidi's unwavering strength that night that set the tone for the kids to be able to withstand the eight-month journey that followed.

I can't even recall how the kids reacted; just Heidi's composure and her absolute faith in her ability to heal and to beat the cancer. I watched her in awe. That is the essence of who Heidi was—a dedicated mother and wife who would move mountains to stay with her loved ones. And for eight months, that's precisely what she did.

Fast forward to the middle of Heidi's chemo treatment schedule only three months later—three treatments down, three to go. (Each chemo session actually consisted of three separate treatments spread over three days.) We celebrated Madeline's bat mitzvah and waited to hear medical updates until after—Heidi wanted to be present and focused on Madeline on her big day.

Heidi's fourth chemo treatment began the following Monday, and we were scheduled to meet with the doctor about the cat scan results during that treatment. I clearly remember walking to the examination room, my heart pounding with anticipation, palms sweaty, mouth dry. As I held Heidi's hand, I could feel the fear running through her body. We said nothing as we walked through the halls to where we'd hear the results.

Going into that situation, we told ourselves that everything would be positive, that the struggles of the previous three months had been worth it, that Heidi's dream and determination to beat cancer was right on target. As we sat down and waited for the doctor, I began to prepare myself, as Heidi's support person. I readied myself for the possibility of hearing that Heidi's cancer had not improved with treatment. I looked over at Heidi and contemplated how I would comfort her if we heard that news; I considered how I might also comfort myself.

As our usually poker-faced doctor began to reveal the results, her voice was elevated, and there was a palpable sense of joy in her expression. She told us that the chemotherapy was not just working, it was working remarkably well; even she was surprised. The smaller tumors had disappeared entirely, and the larger ones had shrunk substantially. For the first time since the ordeal began, we had real, concrete results to back up Heidi's hope.

At the end of May 2015, Heidi completed her final scheduled chemotherapy. The light at the end of the tunnel had never shone so brightly, though Heidi and I had very different reactions. Based on the progress we had seen from the earlier CAT scan, three full treatments ago (and nine individual chemo days), I was confident that the chemo had done its job and the oncologist would tell Heidi she was cancer-free. I was filled with excitement and eager to step back into our lives, and in anticipation of Heidi's recovery and as a reward for the effort it took to get there, I had made a reservation for Disneyland for the end of July. Disneyland was such a happy place for our family; it was the ideal place to celebrate Heidi's victory over cancer. Yet on that "final" day of chemo, Heidi was much more subdued and not convinced it was the end of the road. Physically, she didn't feel cancer-free.

When it was time to hear the results of the post-treatment scan, the oncologist's previous giddiness was not present. She wasted no time, telling us simply that most of the cancer was gone; however, there were still several larger tumors that hadn't disappeared. As long as the tumors remained, they were a threat. She explained that the tumors appeared to be inactive and could remain that way, but they could get active again. The doctor told us Heidi could choose to have two more chemo treatments and continue to work on the tumors—even though she'd been told early on that her body couldn't handle much more than six chemo rounds—but there were no guarantees that even two more treatments would eliminate the cancer completely.

The news didn't just take the wind out of our sails, it put holes in our boat, and we were taking on water. The weight of that decision was immense. The thought of her having to endure two more chemo sessions and all the side effects that came with them was gut wrenching. Having to continue the fight for another six weeks was like adding twenty more years to an already long prison sentence. Heidi's decision to proceed was a true test of her commitment. I canceled Disneyland, and Heidi prepared for more chemo.

By the end of August, just three months later, Heidi's situation began to change dramatically. After she had been on the additional chemo treatment for two weeks with a new doctor, we went to hear the results. Heidi was so weak she could barely move. She needed to be pushed into the office with a wheelchair. It didn't take long into that appointment for the doctor to recognize Heidi's condition. He assessed her visually with a look of great concern on his face. The doctor theorized that there was a blockage in Heidi's liver that was causing jaundice, and she was admitted to the hospital for tests.

It was during that stay that the walls of hope crumbled. The following morning, our doctor told us that the blockage in Heidi's liver was, in essence, uncorrectable and had been caused by the cancer. He then rattled us to the core, discussing the possibility that we might lose the battle. Heidi's liver and kidneys had sustained significant damage. Her liver would not improve until she was able to receive more chemo to shrink the tumors and clear the blockage, but she couldn't receive more chemo unless either her liver or her kidneys improved. Without chemotherapy, there was nothing more that could be done. The doctor outlined a strategy to help the kidneys through hydration and assured us he still had some tricks up his sleeve. This was on Thursday, August 27. Four days later, Heidi would be gone.

I began to realize that Heidi was most likely going to die. I knew in my heart that it was a tall order to expect both her kidneys and her liver to make a miraculous recovery. Nevertheless, I still had a job to do, which was to keep Heidi positive. I had to remain present.

After Heidi was released from the hospital the next day, on Friday, August 28, we went home with a single purpose: to keep Heidi hydrated, making sure she consumed at least one liter of fluid per day. One liter is the equivalent of just two 16.9-ounce bottles of water, the size that is dispensed from an average vending machine. This was a huge challenge, as anything liquid was making Heidi aggressively nauseated. I threw myself into that purpose and made it my mission, somehow still clinging to even the smallest thread of hope that if we could just keep her hydrated, maybe the situation would turn around.

That was the mask I wore on the outside, but on the inside I was unraveling. What made it worse was that, because of Heidi's determination to stay positive, I felt I could not share my feelings of doubt with anyone—not Heidi's mom, not the kids, and certainly not Heidi. It was the most alone and despairing I had ever felt up to that point. I was the captain of our ship, and I couldn't let anyone know we were sinking.

Twenty-four hours later I had to get out and be by myself for a little bit. Heidi was extremely weak and struggling with the ability to be self-sufficient around the house. She could barely get out of bed, and she didn't have the strength to go to the bathroom on her own. While Heidi's mom stayed with her that Saturday, August 29, I drove to a nearby pharmacy that carried a large selection of the medical devices Heidi would need to function at home.

After my floundering descriptions to the pharmacist of what I was looking for, I began to explain that the items were for my wife, who was battling cancer. I could barely complete the sentence, and I became unable to speak anymore. I was a grown man wiping tears off my face in the middle of a pharmacy, in front of a total stranger.

I purchased everything I could think of, not wanting to leave anything behind that might be helpful to Heidi. The pharmacist looked at my bags and offered to help me to my car. Once there, she asked if it would be all right if she gave me a hug. I was taken aback by her request, but also found it quite comforting. As she embraced me, she told me what a good job she thought I was doing, and that she would pray for me, my wife, and my children. Once again I cried, this time on the shoulder of a stranger. This random act of kindness and compassion by someone I had never met before was exactly what I needed in that moment. In the absence of hope, comfort and kindness go a long way toward soothing a broken spirit.

When I returned home, I was still emotional but didn't want Heidi to see my concerns. I told Heidi I needed to go to the mall to make a return, which I did. I kissed my wife goodbye and went on my way. Before I left, Madeline asked if she could come with me. I told her no, I just need some "me" time, and off I went. I didn't get far when the stress of my situation and the emotions of the day overwhelmed me. I began to sob heavily. The fifteen-minute drive to the mall seemed to take hours.

I don't consider myself a spiritual person, and I am not a big believer in God, but on that drive I started a conversation out loud. I said, "If you have to take her, please take her quickly." I knew she couldn't bear to go through an end game of suffering, without hope for a future with me and the kids. I also knew I couldn't handle seeing her suffer physically and emotionally. If it had to end, it would be a blessing for all of us to have it end quickly. After I said that, I couldn't believe what I had spoken. I had put my thoughts into the universe and there was no taking them back.

I often wonder if I did more than just speak my mind that day. I wonder if, at that very moment, I set something in motion that would in fact play out the way I suggested within forty-eight hours. For eight months, I had trained myself to be a fighter and a cheerleader. In less than a week, I had begun to learn a new way of existing—surrender. I allowed thoughts of being alone and of being a single father to enter my mind. I felt as though I had to begin to accept our situation and let go of the hope that had been the driving force in my life for such a long time. I had to prepare for the inevitable. Still, I thought I would have more time to come to terms with those thoughts. I believed that Heidi would at least live through September, if not some of October.

She never heard, two days later, "There is nothing more we can do medically." And she never completely lost hope.

Chapter 3

The Night I Never Left

Heidi and I always laughed about the two of us having met in a bar, as we rarely drank. We were there with mutual friends, and she was sitting right next to me, a very attractive brunette whose long dark hair framed her face and formed a little outward curl just atop her shoulders. She wasn't glammed up or wearing much makeup, which I liked. I leaned over and put my hand out to introduce myself.

"Hi there. I'm Gregg," I said.

"Heidi," she answered.

I remember joking to break the ice, and after that the conversation flowed easily. She laughed a lot, we played a game of pool, and at the end of the night we exchanged business cards with our phone numbers on them. By the time I met Heidi, I had grown tired of the hunt; dating felt like a chore. When after a day or two I hadn't heard from Heidi, I called her. She invited me to a break-the-fast dinner she was hosting at her parents' house, which traditionally follows the Jewish holiday of Yom Kippur.

The night of Heidi's dinner party, the ride up to her house seemed to take forever. I couldn't believe she lived so far away, and I began to wonder if I had missed a turn. Back then, the way to get to Heidi's house was to drive until you thought you'd gone too far and then continue for about ten minutes more.

I approached the front door nervously; some part of me must have known how much my life would change after that night. I took a deep breath and pushed the doorbell. The door opened, and there Heidi was. She smiled and welcomed me with a quick hug. The smell of homemade chicken soup greeted me, and as I entered, I walked past dining tables adorned with fine linens and place settings ready for guests. The kitchen island was covered with food—way more food than could have possibly been consumed by the small crowd of twenty.

I recognized several people from the night at the bar, which was comforting. I met Heidi's parents, some friends of theirs, and Heidi's grandmother, who also lived there. Although Heidi's then boyfriend was also present, as I later learned, Heidi and I spent a good portion of the evening chatting together.

There was a generalized buzz in the air, the kind that's made up of multiple conversations coming together. The perfect hostess, Heidi flitted from group to group, making sure to chat with everyone. However, she still found time to sit with me, mostly on lounge chairs in the backyard away from the crowd. We laughed and we talked.

After several hours, the evening began to wind down, and people started to leave. I wasn't ready to go; I was engulfed in that happy feeling you get at the very beginning of a relationship. I began to help Heidi, bringing dishes into the kitchen, wiping down tables, and helping to wrap and put away extra food. While assisting, I had a chance to get to know Heidi's mother, Judy. Here is a bit of advice: if you want to be successful in dating a Jewish girl, get to know—and charm—her mother first. Soon, only Heidi, her grandmother, her parents, and I remained. After a time and with a puzzled look, Heidi's grandmother said to Heidi's mother, "Who is this guy, and when is he going to leave?"

"The Night I Never Left" started what became an eighteen-year courtship and marriage, but it all ended on August 31, the day Heidi was taken from me by a horrible, fast-moving cancer.

Chapter 4

Pillows

As the last ounce of energy drained from my body that night, I had no choice but to prepare myself to go to sleep alone for the first time in over sixteen years. I looked at my bed and saw the ramp of pillows still lined up against the wall that just this morning had supported Heidi as she rested there. She was gone now, but her pillows remained, untouched. My king-size bed appeared before me like a continent where I could stretch out my arms for miles and never reach the edges. It had lost the inviting sense of comfort that had been present just last night. In less than a day, my bedroom had become foreign to me.

I had no idea what to do next or where to turn.

Part Two

Minus One

Chapter 5

Keeping It Together

September 1, 2015, 6:00 a.m. (Day 1)

Thanks to all for your kind words and thoughts. Heidi was a special lady. . . . Facebook was such a large part of her life. It was the way that she could individually connect to so many. I am sure she is reading all your posts and is grateful for them. . . . Thank you.

September 3, 2015, 9:58 p.m. (Day 3)

Today we laid Heidi to rest.

It was a very tough day.

It was a beautiful September morning. The sun was shining, and there were few clouds in the sky. It was warm, and there was a slight breeze blowing, cooling me in my suit and tie. People were gathered everywhere, some sitting and others standing. They weren't there for a concert or to see a parade or catch a glimpse of someone famous; this was Heidi's funeral.

After a short service, the rabbi gestured toward the pallbearers, and eight women—the women most important in Heidi's life—came forward and surrounded Heidi and three more of her closest friends, supporting her one last time, pushing the wheeled cart that held the casket, moving her along to her final resting place.

Graveside, the crowd around me blurred and faded away outside of my peripheral vision. Stunned and frozen by anguish, I placed my hand on Heidi's casket, longing for one last connection. In that moment it was just the two of us. As the casket lowered, it released itself from the touch of my hand, suspended in the air. Letting go made it real. It felt like the bones in my body had been instantly removed. The sadness inside overtook me; uncontrolled and in front of hundreds, I cried out in a loud shriek. I felt as if my grief filled the air for miles. Inch by inch, Heidi moved down into the earth, farther and farther away from where I stood. I turned to the rabbi next to me and buried my face in his chest; I was lost.

When Heidi had been hospitalized to receive her first chemo treatment, our rabbi and our cantor visited her hospital room. The rabbi had wrapped his tallit, or personal prayer shawl, around Heidi and me and recited the prayer for healing. Then the cantor, ever so softly and oh so beautifully, sang that same prayer. This quiet, poignant moment brought tears to our eyes and made us feel we weren't alone in this battle.

Now I watched as Heidi reached the bottom. Her journey had ended, but mine was just beginning. This was where she would remain, and I had to walk away and return to the tattered remnants of my life.

September 6, 2015, 7:40 a.m. (Day 6)

How do you move on?

You just do.

Every day, when I awake to my quiet house I look around and wonder: How do I get through today? How do I move into the next stage of my life and my children's lives without my wife, without my children's mom, without my best friend?

Today is the sixth day since Heidi passed; I still can't believe it. We are all living in such a different world. As I have expressed to many, I have been blessed to see my sweet Heidi through the eyes of the hundreds of people she has touched. The support and the emotions of others have helped to bring me through this week.

This week has also been a discovery of anatomy. I never knew the human body could generate so many tears and yet still have the ability to create more. I like to believe, as I said at Heidi's funeral, that every tear I shed is a sign of love for her, and I and many others have truly filled an ocean. Every time I cry, I'm giving my sweet wonderful Heidi a hug and assuring her that the kids and I will be okay.

After that fated phone call in December 2014 from her oncologist, we all moved on with Heidi. And now we have to move on without her.

Chapter 6

A Week

September 7, 2015, 7:36 a.m. (Day 7)

I cannot believe it has been one week since Heidi left us.

I have been living in such a surreal world. I've been surrounded by people and yet completely alone. I have been on a different timeline where days and dates have no meaning.

Last night at our shiva service the rabbi was speaking about Heidi, like he has done several times before, and then he mentioned that tomorrow will mark one week since Heidi's passing. I was shocked to hear that because I have lost all sense of time. I began to reflect on last Sunday night when Heidi and her brother, Chad, were sharing a Face-Time call and admiring their matching, very short hairstyles. She was so happy in that conversation; who knew that would be their last?

September 7, 2015, 9:20 a.m. (Day 7)

You should know that the cemetery printed two hundred programs and they ran out.

My family and I arrived at 9:45, the service was due to start at 10:00, and there was a line of cars and overflow parking already in use. We were early to arrive and already late.

All the seats were taken, and it was standing room only.

The rabbi did an amazing job, including reading a poem titled "A Woman of Valor," and something else very special happened: the cantor, who is no longer with our temple, flew in to be there for Heidi and to help officiate this service. Her voice was stunning as always. What a tribute—thank you. I wish all who wanted to could have attended. I know she felt everyone's presence, whether they were physically there or not.

I want to share with you all the eulogy I wrote for Heidi, which the rabbi read so beautifully:

On Monday the world lost a ray of light. The world is a lesser place without her. My world is a lesser place without her.

What can I say about Heidi? How do you describe a super person?

Heidi was the poster child of "do the right thing." That was her motto, no matter what. She was a role model for humanity.

Heidi was the type of person who remembered everyone's name, as well as what you were wearing when you met her.

Heidi helped everybody.

Heidi was a fighter. When she was diagnosed back in December, she said that she would do anything and go through anything to beat cancer and to stay with her family. That was always the force that drove her.

She was never going to give up, no matter what. Even last week when things started to take a turn, she told her brother, Chad, "Don't count me out." She felt as long as there was hope, there was a chance. When Heidi left this world, she left with hope in her heart, not despair.

Every tear shed here today and every tear that will be shed in the future, may be a tear of sadness shed by those of us she leaves behind, but for her, every tear is a drop of love for the most amazing wife, daughter, sister, and mother that I have ever met. The amount of love that will be generated by those she knew and those she touched will fill an ocean. Heidi was a one-of-a-kind human being, and I was privileged to share my life with her.

Heidi was a fantastic writer and editor. She had an eye for things. She could identify if something was crooked by even just the slightest bit, she got a kick out of finding typos in expensive corporate advertising, and she taught all of us that "nother" is not a word.

She would always tell me and our children that we are intelligent people and we should sound like it. She was such a good editor that she was able to edit my driving, my outfits, or the outfits of the kids and pretty much everything in our daily lives.

Heidi's greatest joy was our family. For Heidi, family was everything. Heidi would make sure that dinner waited on nights I had to work late, so we could eat together. She loved picking up the kids from school and hearing about their day. Everything that went on in our lives was important to her.

Heidi was the type of person who would give up everything she had in order to give to others. For us, money was never something we had in abundance, but she would always donate to someone's cause. She would always participate in a dinner for someone, or send flowers to someone who needed them, and the amounts were always more than I was comfortable with. To her it was about lifting someone up or openly supporting someone. For her, it was doing the right thing. Heidi made all of us better people.

Since she was diagnosed, I knew this day might come. Knowing about it and going through it are two totally different things. Without Heidi, there is a huge void left in our family. I am heartbroken. I know that although she is no longer physically with us, she will be in our lives forever.

Madeline, Jack, and Max: You need to know that your mother loved you more than anything. The three of you were the most important people in her life. She was so proud of all three of you. It meant so much to your mom that even though you fought like siblings do and someone usually ended up crying, the three of you have a close relationship like the one she shared with her brother, Chad. The three of you also need to know that your mom will be with you forever. She will always be protecting you. Know that if I let you ride your bikes, near traffic, to the park, she will never like that. She will always be your mom, and you will feel her love for you inside for the rest of your lives. Today is not the end of your mother. Today is the beginning of a new relationship with her.

Heidi, my life will be so much less without you. It will not be easy, but you should not worry. I will take care of our children and your mother as I promised so you don't have to worry about them. I will continue your legacy and try to always do the right thing, even if the right thing is not easy. I love you more than all the stars in the sky. I miss you so much already. Rest in peace, my beloved Heidi.

Chapter 7

Learning to Walk

September 9, 2015, 7:11 a.m. (Day 9)

Last night ended the shiva, our family's official period of mourning according to the Jewish religion. Today marks the beginning of a lifetime of mourning.

The shiva began immediately after the funeral. It lasted six days and gave us an opportunity to be taken care of by our friends and community. It brought therapy to my home in the form of food and company. In a time of vulnerability, we had people there to guide, support, feed, and love us. For one week, while going through a period of intense grief, we were not alone. A funeral is about the deceased; the shiva is about the living.

Each night, the rabbi arrived and conducted a short service. Heidi's popularity brought dozens of people to the shiva; my house was bursting. Each night, dinner was catered, which was organized and paid for by others. Some joined us for dinner and then, shortly after, the masses began to arrive.

The only task I was responsible for was the daily replenishment of ice in the ice chests and making sure they were then filled with sodas and waters. I had nothing to do during the day and couldn't handle much, but this menial task kept me grounded and gave me purpose. It was just enough to keep me planted in reality. I was oddly grateful for the responsibility. This was the only routine we had for a week. There was nothing pending and nowhere to go. There was no work or school; the days blended together. Thursday was like Wednesday, which was like Saturday, which was like Monday.

For one week, the shiva transplants you into a different dimension. It's the only tracker of time you have. It throws you into a revolving door of people coming in and out of your life. Every night, after dinner and before the service, I found myself in my bedroom away from everyone going through a pre-game ritual. I had to take deep breaths and psych myself up to face the crowds in my living room; each individual was there to have their own private interaction with me. They sought me out the moment I entered the room. Walking through the double doors of my room was like emerging through a tunnel and onto the field in front of thousands of screaming and cheering fans, only, to my dismay, the fans were silent, and all eyes were on me. In the place of a celebration were obligation and grief.

Once I emerged, I was on parade, in the spotlight, and everyone was looking for me. I was the bumble bee flying from flower to flower and person to person. With each step I would be face to face with another human experience of grief. Each encounter was the same. It began with a look into my eyes and perhaps a slight tilt of the head, a hug of various lengths, and then, "I am so sorry. Heidi was such a wonderful person. How are you holding up? If you need anything just ask." And then, sometimes, another hug. Everyone was at a different point in their grief. I was trying desperately to move forward in mine, even if just by a few inches. Others were at the beginning of their process. With each hug, I was absorbed and transported to wherever in this journey the one hugging me was. Many times, they would be further behind me, and, therefore, I would take a step backward in my progress to help comfort them. By the time it was over, I had run a marathon, swum the English Channel, and completed the Tour de France. I was exhausted.

As difficult as it was to face the masses every evening, this nightly routine supported and propelled me through the beginning of my journey, when the loss was at its sharpest and most unbearable. For six nights, others held me up when I didn't have the strength to stand on my own two feet. For six nights, my family and I were taken care of. When it was over and I emerged from the blur, a week and a half had gone by. I had some distance from the day of Heidi's passing, and that distance brought some healing. The Jewish religion really figured it out with the shiva.

My house will no longer host dozens of people coming over to pay their respects. No more black ribbon to be worn on my clothing. The symbols of mourning have stopped; the reality of mourning now begins.

It has been one week and two days since Heidi passed, and it seems like a lifetime ago. Every day is filled with moments of remembrance and moments of sadness.

There is no joy in my life. There is no comfort in my home. Everything feels like a foreign place. Every day is different from before. There is a void and an emptiness that fills the space around me.

My beloved wife has been taken away, and I don't know why. Why did such a positive light need to be extinguished? Why did this grief have to come to my family? I know these are questions I cannot truly ask as I will never get the answers. I will hug my children close and help them through this period, as they will help me.

Today we begin a new journey by ourselves. I know there is a ton of support and everyone is willing to step up and help us with whatever we need, and for that I am truly grateful, but this is a path that only we can walk. This journey is a path that only time can make better. We will walk it as a family. We will move on, and we will be okay, but maybe not today. Today is something different.

September 9, 2015, 9:05 p.m. (Day 9)

As you might have been able to predict by my post this morning, today has been a tough day. I found it most interesting that today was overcast, cloudy, and lacking sunlight. That would describe my mood as well as the weather. Chad and his family will be leaving tomorrow, and the reality of our new routine is becoming stronger and more prominent. Our distractions are leaving, and we are left to navigate this road on our own. It is tough. Tonight we got out of the house for dinner. We went to the same restaurant we went to with Chad and the kids when they were here just a few weeks ago. Same restaurant, dramatically different experience. I know that all experiences will now be different. I hate different.

Learning to live with grief on my own is like learning to walk all over again. As the distraction of having others around disappears, I feel a great emptiness that seems only to expand with every passing moment, and moving forward becomes like walking through deep mud. You keep moving, but every step fights you.

I can count on one hand the number of times throughout my sixteen-year marriage I was truly by myself. Now and then I had to go out of town on a business trip, but those occasions were few in number. Heidi and I never vacationed separately; there were no guys' trips or girls' weekends. We never had the desire to be apart. Even the mundane, we did together. When the kids were younger, their Saturday mornings were occupied with tennis lessons. While they were entertained, Heidi and I would pick up groceries or make a Costco run. It never mattered what we did, we always did it together. I was lucky enough to have been able to share my life with my best friend, and we never grew tired of each other. Now, for the first time, I have to face my days alone. I feel as though I'm stranded in my own life, a castaway. The isolation is over-whelming. I will have to reinvent myself and discover how to exist alone.

In the past, I never paid attention to what it took to keep our growing family organized on a daily basis; Heidi had that under control. Dinners magically showed up on our table every night. Paperwork for children's activities were filled out and turned in. Homework and school projects got done. Heidi managed our family with great skill; she made it look effortless. In an instant, everything I'd never paid attention to, like passwords, dinner menus, grocery lists, and school functions, has become my responsibility. All that had been comfortable has become uncomfortable. Just being the driver is no longer good enough. Now, her tasks are my tasks. I have huge shoes to fill, and my feet feel tiny in comparison.

Looking toward tomorrow I have to face my fears: The fear of being without a relationship. The fear of being a single parent. The fear of not knowing how to lessen the pain, for myself or my kids. I have to choose how I want to live and carry on. I will have to relearn everything, and I'm not sure I have the strength.

Nonetheless, the clock keeps ticking. Our world has stopped, but the world around us is still moving. I don't have the luxury of hiding in a corner curled up into a ball, watching life go on without me. I have three kids who now need me more than ever. I have to show up for them. This has become my rallying cry.

Chapter 8

My Kids

September 10, 2015, 10:13 p.m. (Day 10)

Tonight I am so proud of my kids. I thought today was going to be the third tough day we had to get through. First was the day Heidi passed, second was her funeral, and then there was today. Today the hype is over, and we are alone.

Chad and his family flew back to Portland. Today was just Judy, me, and the kids. Tonight will be our first dinner at our table with an empty chair where Heidi once sat. For days I've been wondering, how will we get through this?

After Chad's crew left, I took a deep breath. My kids went on a bike ride together, then they came home and went swimming. They stayed together as if to reassure themselves that they would be okay.

Today Madeline, Jack, Max, and I got back to the mundane. Simple things, but really big steps. We went grocery shopping. When dinnertime arrived, Judy and I asked the kids if they thought we should remove the leaf from our table so we could be closer together and maybe lessen the impact of an empty chair. The kids said no, leave it alone; if we have people over, we can use the big table.

My kids are amazing! I was so worried about them and about what today would bring. They were so great and are showing such strength. Seeing them manage allows me to manage.

Madeline, Jack, and Max: my kids. They are the fuel that powers my existence. They are the reason not just to carry on, but to thrive. Every day, I look at my children, and they give me reassurance that we can continue to move forward, intact and as a family.

Madeline is our firstborn and is everything I would have hoped for in a girl. She has been blessed with long, curly hair, which she loves to braid, and a wonderful dark complexion. She has always worn very little makeup and radiates a natural beauty.

Like her mother, she has developed a love of baking. Although she's not quite the pastry chef just yet, I'm sure that over time and with more practice the cake mixes will be traded for ingredients to bake from scratch.

In many ways, watching Madeline grow up has been like seeing Heidi's personality reflected in a mirror. Like her mother, Madeline is a rule follower, even when no one is watching. Madeline has her mother's memory. She can memorize hundreds of vocabulary words and definitions for school. She makes lists and tracks important dates, like my mother's birthday, so I don't forget to call her. She remembers everyone's birthday—friends, relatives, friends' parents—even pets. Remembering all the birthdays and anniversaries had always been Heidi's job, and Madeline has stepped right into her mother's shoes, channeling Heidi.

Also like Heidi, Madeline has a powerful work ethic. She spends hours on homework and days completing projects and studying for exams. Like a runner training for a marathon, she attacks each task with strong will and determination, every bit her mother's daughter.

A short twenty months after Madeline, we welcomed Jack into our family. At a very early age it became clear that Jack was remarkably intelligent. By his first birthday he was speaking in complete sentences and had a vocabulary of almost 150 words—far beyond that of the average child his age. At three, when we began to teach his big sister how to read, he joined in and taught himself. Jack remains an intellectual.

Throughout elementary and middle school, he's never received a grade lower than an A. Success in school comes easy to him.

As blessed as he was with his intelligence, at age four, Jack was given a diagnosis that would shape and challenge him for the rest of his life—Type 1 diabetes. Heidi and I had to hold him down to administer insulin, via syringe. I couldn't look him in the face. As I heard his unanswered cries for help, I began to cry. Jack's reactions were more than Heidi could bear, so I became the administrator of insulin and the one to check his blood sugar initially.

Jack's diagnosis matured him quickly, thrusting him out of a normal childhood. Because diabetes requires constant monitoring and management, he had to deal with things that other children his age didn't. He had to be accompanied by either Heidi or me at every drop-off party or event. He was rarely invited to other boys' houses for playdates because their parents feared the responsibility. He was often singled out and isolated when food situations arose. Jack continues to be both more cautious than his siblings and mature beyond his years.

Heidi had always envisioned a family with three children, while I was completely content with our perfect family of four. We fit nicely into any size booth or table at a restaurant, I didn't need a big SUV with extra seating, and we could easily manage just one room in a hotel. Of course, that was not to be. Just as we were settling in with two toddlers, several pregnancy tests would announce the arrival of our third child, Max.

It's funny to look back at the challenges of having multiple children. Having our first child was taxing. We knew nothing about parenting, and Madeline's colic tested our patience. Every day seemed difficult—until we had Jack. With the arrival of our second child, having only one seemed ridiculously easy. Having two children under the age of three and managing all their needs felt nearly impossible to keep up with. Then we had Max, and having only two children seemed simple by comparison. With Max we had three children under the age of five, and suddenly we were outnumbered. Thankfully, we decided to not make three easy by having a fourth.

Max bore little resemblance in personality to either his brother or his sister. Where Madeline and Jack were the scholars of the family, Max was the creative free-thinker. As a toddler, he was perfectly happy on his own within his imagination. He locked himself in his room and dressed up in superhero costumes to save the world. We nicknamed him "Messy Max" because he got into everything and left a trail of destruction behind him. We often found him sitting on the kitchen floor next to an open drawer, Ziploc storage bags strewn around him and an entire roll of aluminum foil unraveled like a red carpet. He liked to scatter placemats and plastic plates around as if leaving a trail so he could be found at a later date. His greatest moment, however, came with the assistance of his older brother. Jack decided it would be fun to open a jar of peanut butter. Max took Jack's idea to a higher level. Heidi walked into our bedroom and found Messy Max on the floor in front of our TV wearing nothing but peanut butter and a diaper. Peanut butter covered his face in streaks. His chest was covered, and so were his legs; he wore the peanut butter like lotion all over his body. The TV and its stand were finger-painted in peanut butter, and the carpet around him was saturated. Heidi, thankfully, took several photos of the crime scene.

Max is the most sensitive and outwardly emotional of the three. He's a hugger. Before you leave Max, he is always good for a hug and an "I love you."

In many ways, my children are just like everyone else's children. They're social and enjoy time with their friends. They play sports and shop. They work hard in school and get good grades. They play video games and watch Netflix and YouTube. Yet just below the surface they are anything but normal. They have endured a loss no child should ever have to endure. They have seen and experienced things that set them apart from their friends. They face their pain with strength and dignity, the likes of which many adults are incapable of. When Heidi was laid to rest, our children's innocence was buried with her.

Heidi, we did a good job with these kids. You can rest easy knowing they are going to get through this, maybe even better than we both might have thought. You would be so proud of them. Don't worry, we will all be okay. We got this.

Good night, I love you. ❤

Chapter 9

The Weight of the World

September 11, 2015, 8:51 p.m. (Day 11)

How much does the weight of the world weigh?

Today, it seems I found out. I knew today would come, the kind of day that no matter what you do, it doesn't matter. This was the kind of day immersed in a heaviness I couldn't carry.

I took the kids to Topgolf to get them out of the house; the more distracted they are the better they seem to be. We had a nice time, but it felt insincere.

From time to time, Madeline has talked to me about how much she "hates" something. I always look at her and say, "'Hate' is such a strong word. How about 'strongly dislike'?" Well, I've gotta tell you, I hate that Heidi is gone, I hate being a single father of three, and I hate being a family of four when we have always been a family of five.

Today, even the little tasks seemed huge and overwhelming. Heidi carried so much for our family. She had everything organized; she kept us moving; she knew what, when, and where. She was the hardest working non-paid person I knew. How do you fill such shoes? You don't.

Tonight we all went back to Shabbat services at our temple. This was tough. We were at Shabbat because after the shiva and for the next thirty days a Jewish family is encouraged to come to the synagogue, be supported publicly, and say the Kaddish, or mourner's prayer. It's an opportunity to be surrounded by community and, together, help uplift Heidi's soul to a higher place.

As Judy, the kids, and I walked into the sanctuary, I felt people following us with their eyes. I was now the congregation's picture of what grief looked like, and I felt a strange pressure to perform. How was I supposed to act? To look? Could I smile, could I cry? With each step, I felt as though I was being scanned and analyzed. I was on display and people were lined up to see me.

It was hard to sit and look around the room and see the families in attendance. Everywhere I saw a mother, father, and kids. It was isolating. I looked at their kids, and then looked at mine. I hoped that my kids were not seeing the same thing I was.

The rabbi talked about putting good out into the world and getting good back. He talked about making a choice to help someone who needs help because it's the right thing to do. All I could think about was that this was how Heidi had lived every day.

Heidi was the epitome of doing the right thing, always taking time to be truly present and talk to the "uh-huh" people—those surface listeners who mostly nod their heads and say "uh-huh." She always looked beneath to see what was inside someone. She never forgot a birthday or special occasion, sending cards or money even for unusual occasions, like when a friend's daughter had her birthday money stolen from her bag at school, and Heidi gave her $20 without a second thought. Heidi's note to the mother: "I want Hayleigh to feel like there's goodness in the world, too. I want to take what is an upsetting day and make it brighter."

She helped anyone who needed it, she put good everywhere, and of course she always did the right thing. Her reward for living this way was a non-survivable cancer. In my head, Heidi's epitaph reads, "Do the right thing and get paid back with cancer." Perhaps I feel a little bitter. Perhaps I feel that life is a little unfair. Perhaps I am just having a very bad day. . . . I know that not all days will be like today, and that not all days will suck, but today did.

Chapter 10

The Roller Coaster

September 12, 2015, 8:20 a.m. (Day 12)

Today is another day, and so far it seems better. However, the day is still young. This road I now travel is not so much a road, as a roller coaster. It raises you up only to drop you down a steep incline. It has twists and turns and throws you upside down. I feel my body and head being bounced around with every passing yard. You are strapped in and secured, but you never feel safe. I usually like roller coasters, but not this one. Most roller coasters are over relatively quickly; I fear I will be on this one for quite some time.

I am planning to take the kids to Disneyland next month. Heidi loved Disneyland. She felt it was truly the Happiest Place on Earth. We went there often as a family, and we have many wonderful memories. I'm sure "It's a Small World" will feel very different. But there is no question that our family can use some happy.

September 13, 2015, 6:58 a.m. (Day 13)

The time has come to start cleaning a house that isn't dirty. Yesterday, Judy and I began the task of going through the house and removing

Heidi's things. This is a day I knew had to come, but I have been dreading it.

For poor Judy, this is not the first time she has had to do something like this. In April 2014, Ira, her husband of fifty-two years, passed away. As hard as this is for her, I am grateful to have her by my side to help guide me down this emotional path.

We began the sorting process in my pantry, where there was an entire shelf of cookbooks. Heidi loved her cookbooks and had many of them. She had more meals and desserts in these books than anyone could possibly consume in a lifetime. She had cake books, cupcake books, diabetic meal books, and books filled with low-calorie meals. She had Paula Dean, the Barefoot Contessa, and so many more. Old books, new books, hardcover, paperback, and everything in between. She had six three-ring binders of recipes she collected over the years. There were countless times that she found a recipe on some website and emailed it to me to print and bring home; they were all there, too.

Judy and I were left with this inheritance. What do we do? Someone already started a food network, so that's out. Our choice was clear. It was time to remove the collection. I know this was a logical decision, but it didn't make it any easier. I'm sure Heidi was watching us, and I know that she understands, but I'm sure she was wiping off tears as it was happening. I'm sure she's angry that she's no longer here and that we needed to do this. In addition to the cookbooks, Heidi also had some kitchen appliances in there that I will realistically never use. They will go also.

Many will say that this is all part of the healing process and moving forward. Intellectually, I get that, but emotionally, how do you remove someone from your life again? I suppose the pantry was the easy one. The closet is still to come. There is so much Heidi here; she is every-where. I wish I could just wake up and tell Heidi about the bad dream I had, you know, the one where she died of cancer? Unfortunately, this is no dream, and there are things that must be done no matter how hard. Each task erases some of the physical reminders of what was and what can never be again. Heidi is gone, and there is nothing I can do to change that.

September 13, 2015, 4:12 p.m. (Day 13)

Many people are checking in and asking how I am doing. I thought I might say a little something about that. The truth of the matter is I don't know how I am doing. It's a very tough question to answer. I find myself challenged to get through the moments, but not from a standpoint of "OMG I am so damned depressed," because I don't feel that depression has taken over. I find it hard to feel anything.

I can't feel excitement, and I can't feel sorrow. There is a numbness that overtakes me, and it is all-encompassing. Perhaps this is my mind putting up a defense because the emotional pain is way too fresh and would be too great without it. All I know is that I am powerless at this time to change it.

I am living in a fog and that fog makes it challenging to accomplish much of anything. I have plenty of things to get done, but they all seem "way over there," too far to get to. I am looking forward to rejoining the world on Tuesday and going back to work full-time for the first day in a long time. Distractions are good, but they are still just a temporary fix. The solution lies within me, and I will somehow find the strength to move forward. So when you all ask, "How are you?" I guess the answer is "I don't know."

Chapter 11

Firsts

September 13, 2015, 11:08 p.m. (Day 13)

Firsts are so tough. Tonight we experienced two firsts. Tonight I grilled steaks. This by itself is nothing to write about, but for the last sixteen years when I grilled steaks, I would always have to make one well-done. Heidi always ordered her steak well-done; she was the only one in the family who did that. You would be surprised how many places cannot prepare a steak this way. It took a long time to learn to prepare Heidi's steak the way she wanted it, but I finally figured out how. Basically, you cook it normally with the other steaks, and when they are done and you think Heidi's would be done also, cook it longer. There were so many times when there would be a solo steak on the grill. Everyone would be eating, and I would be cooking one steak. Tonight, I did not make a well-done steak.

Jack went to a birthday party at his friend's house today. They live on the west side, about a half-hour away. When I picked him up, he was happy and had had a great time. Then it hit Jack that, for the first time, he wouldn't be able to share his excitement and the details of this party with his mother, who was always interested and excited for him. I could see his mood change. I found myself tearing uncontrollably, feeling and sharing his pain as I, too, realized that I would not be able to share my sadness about his comments with Heidi. We were experiencing different details but sharing the same anguish.

Firsts suck!

September 15, 2015, 9:35 a.m. (Day 15)

Today we go back into the world. The kids go back to school, and I go back to work. What a different world it is.

Jack and Madeline felt like it was the first day of school all over again, even though they had started this school year back in early August. They weren't sure what to expect from their teachers, their friends, or even themselves. After I dropped them off, I went into the office and met with the assistant principal and their guidance counselor. They are great people; they will take care of the kids and make sure they transition back without a hitch. I then went and dropped off Max and met with his administration. Same thing.

As for me, today I return to work for the first time in three weeks, which includes the final week of Heidi's life, when I stayed home with her. I know we all have to rejoin the world, but it's a very strange thing to do. I can't believe it's only been two weeks and a day since Heidi's passing. It feels like a lifetime, although I can remember every second of the Monday morning she passed. Time moves very strangely when one goes through an experience like this. I know today is good, and I know that we have to get through today in order to get to tomorrow, and then I need to get through tomorrow to get to the next day, and so on and so on. How can we truly ever be "normal" again?

September 15, 2015, 8:12 p.m. (Day 15)

Well, we made it. We made it through our first day back in the world full-time. It was okay. Madeline told me that many of her friends reached out and tried to comfort her. Jack had a harder day. He told me that in the middle of math class he started thinking about Mom. It made him very sad. It's hard to focus on school when all you want to do is curl up in a corner and cry.

Both Madeline and Jack said it was really hard to come home and not be able to go into the bedroom and tell Mom about their day. She always wanted to know, and she always genuinely cared. I haven't heard from Max yet, as he was whisked off to football practice before I came home and isn't back yet.

As for me, every day I get reminders of what once was and is no more. My biggest concern about today was lunch. For years, Heidi and I would go out to lunch three, four, or five days a week. We always figured it was too expensive to have date night every week, or she would get too busy with homework or other projects in the evening, so we had lunch. No kids, just us. Even after she got sick, we would still have lunch together as often as we could. I loved lunch. That was our time. Our time to catch up, to talk about the kids, school, work, or whatever.

Today lunch was different. One restaurant came strongly into my head, a place Heidi and I went a lot. We loved the desert cobb salad, and she loved the creamy chicken and rice soup. We both thought they were the best soup and salad in town. Heidi could have soup anytime, even on a hot summer day. We ate there so often the owner knew exactly what we would get: "Two cobbs, two ranch, and one herb Romano vinaigrette," she would say. I flashbacked to where we sat and what we talked about. It was such a simple thing, nothing out of the ordinary or overly special. It was just lunch. A lunch I would give anything to have just one more time.

Normally, we look forward to firsts—the first airplane ride, the first day of school, the first day at a new job. We might feel a little nervous for them, but it is always nervous excitement. Thankfully, a first we didn't have to experience without Heidi was Madeline's bat mitzvah, in March. She was able to stand with me in front of the congregation, across from Madeline, and experience that special moment and the pride and sense of accomplishment our daughter felt.

After losing Heidi, firsts have come to mean something else. Familiar experiences have turned into something completely unfamiliar, something scary and worrisome. A countdown of sorts has begun.

Chapter 12

The Slow Starvation of Grief

September 16, 2015, 7:12 a.m. (Day 16)

Last night was not a great night. Jack's blood sugar numbers were high all night and didn't want to come down. I was awakened many times with a nasty cough. And I had my first dream with Heidi in it.

I wish I could say this dream involved Heidi and me strolling through endless green fields topped with flowers, or the two of us at a kid's graduation, or something fun or romantic like that. But it wasn't.

My dream had Heidi and me showing up together at a grief support group. We went around the room and introduced ourselves, and when it was Heidi's turn, she stood up, said her name, and broke down in a wave of emotion announcing that she had cancer. Later in the dream, I showed up in this group by myself just after Heidi had passed.

It was a tough dream. It was like reliving her loss all over again. Needless to say, I'm pretty tired this morning.

September 16, 2015, 5:19 p.m. (Day 16)

Have you ever been hungry? I mean, starving? So hungry that your stomach aches? Or so thirsty that your throat is parched? So thirsty that you would give anything for just one drop of water?

This has been my day. I've been so hungry and thirsty for a conversation or an interaction with Heidi. I know this comes and goes in waves. Today it was a tidal wave.

I went to work, but that didn't mask it. I went to lunch with friends, but that didn't satisfy the craving. I feel the only thing today that can satisfy the hunger and quench the thirst is something I can't have. This really sucks!

Additionally, I started the awful task of undoing things that were in Heidi's name. I canceled her cell phone number. I put the cable, phone, and internet in my name. This was horrible, not only because of doing the switch from her to me, but because there was a mix-up in the process. In order to switch the phone into my name they have to disconnect our existing line and restart the line under my name. Not a big deal until I realized, while I was on hold in the middle of the process, that Heidi's voice was still on our greeting. I panicked! I felt like I had just slipped off a cliff and begun to fall in slow motion. I was helpless to stop this process.

The customer service representative came back on the line, and it was done. My intention had been to capture her voice on a sound bite and keep her greeting. That was no longer a possibility; her voice was gone. I was devastated. Then I realized that maybe I could get it off her cell phone, but I had canceled that earlier. Gone again. I know it's not a huge deal; I know I have her voice captured in other places. I know, I know. Still, when you only have what you have, and there is no way to duplicate what you lose, everything matters.

Losing her voicemail greeting really messed me up. I can't believe it's been just a little over two weeks without the ability to talk to her, hang out with her, or hold her hand. It feels like a lifetime. The distance is so great. I can't imagine what it will feel like when it has been a month, or two, or three. I cannot see that far. This feeling of being surrounded by people and yet completely by myself is almost more than I can bear. I absolutely HATE it.

September 16, 2015, 5:34 p.m. (Day 16)

OMG!! I am such a mess right now. I can't stop crying. This really blows!

September 17, 2015, 11:01 p.m. (Day 17)

Even simple things can be challenging. For the past week or so, Jack's numbers have been a little out of whack. They have been mostly in the two hundreds and three hundreds. In diabetes talk, that hasn't been very good. Unfortunately, diabetes doesn't care what you are going through emotionally. It has no empathy, and it has its own agenda. I took Jack's pump to his endocrinologist, and he made some adjustments in dosage to fix the problem.

Unfortunately, I had no idea how to program his pump on an ongoing basis. This was one more thing that Heidi always took care of and had under control. Maybe I should have paid more attention and learned the tech side of Jack's pump. Lucky for me, there is an army of diabetes moms (D-moms) out there, and it seems Heidi knew them all. I made a call, and the troops were rallied. Within minutes I had a D-mom calling me who uses the same pump Jack uses, and she walked me through the process to get these adjustments done.

I am so grateful to have the support of so many. Heidi's networking definitely hooked me up. Thanks, D-mom army.

September 18, 2015, 5:04 p.m. (Day 18)

Today I got a text from Tracy, one of Heidi's D-mom friends, telling me that she had a dream last night with Heidi in it, and she was speaking to Tracy reassuring her that everything will be okay in time. I responded to Tracy. She then texted back a one-word response, "Same." Why is this significant? Why did this affect me enough to write about it?

It matters because for many years every email Heidi and I ever wrote to each other would end in "Same." I can't even remember when this started, but one day we were speaking on the phone and ending the conversation; she said, "Goodbye, I love you." I must have been in a public, not-by-myself setting, because I simply responded aloud, "Same." It took her by surprise and she questioned, with a smile, I hope, my choice of words. I explained it, and from then on, we signed every email to each other with "Same." Tracy, thank you for the memory.

Heidi, Same.

September 19, 2015, 6:38 a.m. (Day 19)

I have been awakened to another day where I must deal with the realization that the woman I chose to spend the rest of my life with is no longer here. The woman that I uttered the vows "For better or worse or till death do us part" so long ago, is gone.

Who knew that these vows would be tested? We had the better, we had the worse, and it took death to part us. These days without her seem to last forever.

As I approach the third week since her death it seems as though time moves in an alternate reality. Minutes seem like hours, hours seem like days, and days seem like months. It feels like she has been gone a lifetime. The realization that she is no longer here is beginning to take root.

Everything I do now has a "minus one" sense about it. This is so tough to get used to. When all your friends are couples and you are no longer a couple, it's hard to feel normal. I go through the motions of life but am clouded by an underlying layer of fog that doesn't burn off as the day progresses. My children and I express our disbelief every day. We constantly ask ourselves, Why Heidi? Why us? It doesn't make any sense. When do we find out the purpose of this loss? When do we find out the why?

Today will be another day. Another day with plans, get-togethers, and tasks to be done.

Today will be another day on autopilot where my body will lead my brain and my heart through the motions of the day.

Today, I will be present and not present, all at the same time. I will look like I'm improving on the outside but still be devastated on the inside. I will continue this journey, and I will get through today. I will do all of this because there is no other choice.

Oh, what I would give to have my old, stressed-out, boring life back. Perspective is a crazy thing. Those mundane and necessary trips to the grocery store that you never want to do—what a gift. Errands to buy kids clothing or make returns of clothing you didn't keep—what a gift. Trips to Costco or Sam's Club—what a gift. PTO meetings, school orientations, or meet-the-teacher nights—what a gift. What a gift all these things are when you have someone to share them with.

During Heidi's battle, I often asked myself, if these are going to be our last days together, how do I want to spend them? The answer was, exactly how I did.

Cherish time, because you never know when time will run out.

September 20, 2015, 11:40 p.m. (Day 20)

It is becoming harder to find things to post about. That may be a good thing.

When I started this journey three weeks ago to post my feelings and make my moments public, it was very easy to find words to describe my state of being. The posts flowed from within me to match my grief. Sharing was something I never could have predicted I would do. There is comfort in connecting with others, and I am beginning to understand why this was so important for Heidi.

Today, no post came to mind. What does that mean?

Has my writing potion worn off?

Have I lost my ability to express my feelings?

No, I don't think so.

I think what is happening is that today—day 20—may be the first day that I am feeling an adjustment to this new normal. I say an adjustment, because believe me, I am in no way normal right now. However, today felt like maybe, just maybe, I am getting there.

With each passing day, I find myself getting further and further from my old life. I have to learn ways to handle the enormity of the grief I'm experiencing. I have no idea what to do. I can't hide behind or disguise the feelings of loneliness and devastation, or pretend to be fine. I have to live in the emotions as they appear.

Yet grief is becoming familiar. I am learning how to handle it and co-exist with it. In a sense, I am becoming peaceful in my own misery, moments when the clouds separate and a few rays of sunlight break through. Now don't get me wrong; I can still cry on a dime, and I can still negate this entire post by being a complete wreck tomorrow.

Of course, with this new emotion come questions. How can I feel normal? It has only been three weeks since Heidi's passing. I shouldn't feel normal; I should feel miserable. I should be so far deep in depression that I can't function.

Feeling okay is also triggering a new emotion: guilt. It feels wrong to feel okay and however slightly at peace. It makes me question my relationship and the type of person I am. What kind of ogre feels okay after three weeks?

Throughout this journey my motto has remained clear: "I will let the feeling that becomes present, be present."

There are times in life when we must adjust to a new normal. Having your first child creates a new normal. Losing your wife to cancer does the same. Making the adjustment takes time. Giving birth to Madeline was the beginning of our family. Losing Heidi was the beginning of our new family. Like having a baby for the first time, there is nothing you can do to prepare yourself for the journey; there is no instruction manual, no road map or GPS to follow. You only have your emotions and your instincts, and you have to trust them.

We as a family need to move forward. We need to take baby steps and continue with life. We are living. We need to make plans for the future, and we need to start making new memories. Every step of the day is new. Every minute we breathe is uncharted. We must shape this new future and define what it will look like.

If I am devastated and sad, then it is okay to be devastated and sad. If I am okay, then it is okay to be okay. Today I was okay.

Chapter 13

What Do You Mean, Soon?

September 23, 2015, 6:00 a.m. (Day 23)

I was awakened by images from which I cannot escape. They are the images of Monday morning, August 31, 2015. They've been repeating over and over and over again. These are the images of Heidi's last moments.

Heidi took charge of her situation all the way to the end. Prior to "letting me" call 911, she told me she had questions she wanted me to write down to ask the doctor when we got there. I got a pad and pen, but by that time she was unable to recall what her questions were. I told her that the call had been made, and the paramedics would arrive soon. Knowing she was going to the hospital, she insisted we change her shirt and send her off with a clean one she hadn't slept in.

When the paramedics arrived, she began to take charge of them as well. Now keep in mind these were five big, hunky, girls'-dream-come-true kind of guys. They could handle any situation. When they brought the gurney into our bedroom, Heidi looked at the gurney and felt something about it was not going to work. She said, "I don't mean to be a pain, but can you change the orientation so my head will be at this end?" I have no clue what she was thinking, but these guys backed it out and turned it around for her. Off to the hospital we went.

I remember driving behind the ambulance Heidi was being transported in. It was going very slowly and cautiously—no lights, no sirens, no craziness. The trip to the hospital seemed to take hours. Upon arrival there was no parking near the ER, so I valet parked.

That made sense since I knew Heidi was going to be admitted that day. That part was obvious.

When I finally arrived in the ER, I was taken to the room where Heidi was. Judy was with her. Heidi was struggling with her breathing. The nurse tending to her was trying to calm Heidi down, as she was hyperventilating. By this point, Heidi's jaundice was severe, as if she had a bad spray-on tan. I thought it was weird that only one nurse was with her.

A little later a doctor came in and assessed her. He called Judy and me out into the hallway, a moment I'll never forget. He told us her liver was failing, and he asked if we wanted to initiate extreme measures, i.e., tubes, machines, etc. It was shocking to hear that question. Judy and I both immediately said no.

If there is no potential for a positive outcome, why prolong the suffering? At that point I began to enter an alternate reality.

He told us it would be soon. I remember gagging on those words. I remember asking him, "'Soon'? What do you mean, 'soon'? Can't you stretch it out? Her brother is getting on a plane and will be here early this afternoon. My kids are in school. What do you mean, 'soon'?"

He said, "You might want to go grab the kids and bring them." Right after that, the nurse called the doctor back into the room. Judy and I were out in the hall looking at each other with blank stares. I couldn't believe this was really taking place. Shortly after the doctor went into the room, he came out and told me, "Forget getting the kids; it's happening now."

When I reentered the room, Heidi was no longer sitting up, no longer conscious. She was no longer struggling with her breathing. She was calm and peaceful. I was in shock. What do you do? What do you say? I told her it was okay to go. I told her I would take care of the kids and her mom, like I had already promised, and that she didn't have to worry.

Judy was on one side of her, and I was on the other. We both held on to her, and then she was gone. We had arrived at the hospital at approximately 9:15, Heidi passed at 10:04.

Throughout the entire cancer battle, the one thing Heidi requested of Judy and me was she never be left alone. That was the gift we gave her right up to her very last breath; she was never alone.

It is so hard to get through the days without you, Heidi. Everywhere I go, I see you. I miss you so much. I wish so much that you were still here with us.

—Same.

Chapter 14

Reinventing Life

September 23, 2015, 5:59 p.m. (Day 23)

Life is so strange. Tonight I sat down to do my least favorite task, entering receipts into QuickBooks. I've done this many times before, but tonight this task held a completely different meaning. As I started to enter the receipts one by one, I noticed they all were dated August 30, 2015, the day before Heidi's passing. Even then, life was just life.

On these receipts were simple things like mac 'n' cheese, Balance bars, eggs, and other everyday items. Additionally, I had Propel water, lemonade, and other drinks. I was buying everything I could to try and give Heidi a variety of liquids so she could reach her daily liter of liquid, which was the mission of that weekend. Heidi had been unable to drink regular water without throwing up. So we had to be creative. Another receipt revealed a trip to the local deli to buy her some turkey, as there was very little that she was eating, but she liked that.

As I came across these receipts, my mind wandered back. I found it hard to believe that at the time when I was just getting groceries, I was already in the final countdown with my wife. Looking back at time is so surreal.

As I delved further into the pile, I found several handwritten notes. They read: toner cartridges, clothes for Madeline, Sequoya PTO membership. These stupid little notes were some of the last things Heidi would ever write. We were just living life. Several days later she would be gone.

September 26, 2015, 9:05 a.m. (Day 26)

Last Monday an envelope arrived in the mail. It contained the death certificates for Heidi—another tangible reminder that this is no dream. Getting these are such a shock to the system. They are so official with their embossed seal and large header, "State of Arizona." They even have the decorative border as if to disguise each as a diploma, or a certificate of achievement, or something good that you would frame and hang in your office. Unfortunately, this isn't good. This is just another hard reminder of what was and can never be again.

In these official-looking papers is what a person has been summarized to. But how does a person's forty-eight years of existence come down to a few marks on a paper? Heidi was a great writer, she was a great editor, she loved to bake, travel, spend time with family and friends. Heidi did the very best she could in everything she attempted. She always did the right thing. Heidi was a very patient and caring person with a great sense of humor. Heidi loved romantic comedies and the theater. She loved every *Real Housewives* show from every city. Heidi loved good food, as long as it wasn't on the bone and was well done. She was a great school teacher to our children. She was a supporter of others' causes and a champion of her own. She was a fantastic daughter, sister, and mother, and a most amazing wife. She was so much more than a piece of paper.

Each certificate contributes to physically erasing Heidi's presence in this world—no more life insurance premium to pay, no more health insurance card for her, no more withholding on her paychecks. Everything that was Heidi has come to a complete and sudden stop. It is still just so hard to comprehend.

September 27, 2015, 8:37 a.m. (Day 27)

Although I am starting to understand that everything I do will be on my own, I still have trouble accepting it. I get that I am not alone, that I have three wonderful children and a mother-in-law who fill my world daily, but none of that is the same. The relationship I had with Heidi was one of a kind. We did everything together. She got me. She got my sometimes twisted sense of humor that nobody else got. We talked about everything and about nothing, all the time; about the kids and their activities or their schooling, the victories and stresses of my work, diabetes. We shared dreams and hopes for our future.

Now I have no one to talk to about any of this.

I get what I am supposed to do to keep my family together, that I am it. I can take on this role for others. I can handle it. What I can't handle is how this new world pertains to me and to me alone.

Today the boys and I are going to a Cardinals game, and after, there will be no one to tell about it. In two weeks we will go to Disneyland and there will be no partner to share that with. Every experience I have, I will have by myself. When Heidi and I were engaged, umpteen years ago, my family and I went on the trip of a lifetime to Italy and Greece; Heidi couldn't go. It was a great trip, but I remember feeling lost and empty to all the great things that I was seeing and experiencing, because everywhere we went I could only think of how much Heidi would have loved to be there and to see what I was seeing. I remember how my experience was tainted because I couldn't share it with the one I wanted most to share it with. I would try and call Heidi regularly on the phone from Europe to tell her what I was doing and how much I missed her. Her phone bill that month was in the hundreds. Now I can't pick up the phone and call, though I would pay anything to be able to do so.

I cannot get the days to move more quickly than a snail. I wake up today and can't believe that the date is September 27, another day in September. This has been the longest month of my life. Oh, if I could only see October! Just four short weeks ago, Heidi was still talking to me. She was seeing friends and she was laughing at her brother's jokes. Just four weeks ago—feels like four years.

I keep myself busy, and I keep my family busy, but I can't find my place in this new world. When does this loneliness fade away? When do I feel like myself again? When? If only there were a crystal ball to answer all the questions I have. It's so hard to keep focused at work, to keep on top of everything that has to be done at home. The smallest tasks seem like mountains I have to climb.

I have been almost continuously receiving donation receipts from JDRF (Juvenile Diabetes Research Foundation) from contributions made in Heidi's name, and sympathy cards from so many. Every day I get reminders that this is no dream, this is real. It's so hard to take. It's so hard to read the cards, but yet weirdly comforting at the same time. I think that sums up my emotional status. Every minute is hard—weird and very new. Without the familiar to provide a stable cushion, I have to reinvent every moment, and I am tired of it. It's a lot of work and not the kind of work I get paid for. More effort will not make me wealthy; it's just what I have to do to survive.

I can't shake this, and I can't get time to move normally. I am so tired, and no amount of sleep will see me rested.

I just want my old life back!

September 30, 2015, 9:08 p.m. (Day 30)

Since this Monday it's felt like time is beginning to return to normal. Today I had to pinch myself because I realized it was already Wednesday, and Monday didn't seem like a year ago. I think this means I'm adjusting to my new normal. That life is continuing. That I'm going to be okay.

The boys and I went to the Arizona Cardinals game this past Sunday. In the middle of the game, Jack turned to me and said, "Dad, if Mom was still alive we wouldn't be here." That statement was so profound, especially from my twelve-year-old. He was so right. We were given the tickets by a friend of mine who felt we could use something good. This is a mindset I've been struggling with for a while now—the idea of something positive arising from something so negative. The positive and the negative have been happening at the same time and sharing the same space. My kids have been able to have friends over again, and they couldn't when Heidi was alive because she was just too sick. I've been able to join a gym and start working out with a trainer to improve my health, and I never would have had that in the budget if Heidi were still alive. We were lucky if we were able to go on one vacation a year, and we always had to drive because flying was just too expensive. Now we are going to Disneyland and looking to plan another trip at the end of next spring.

The kids asked me, "Why can we all of a sudden afford these things?" I explained what life insurance was, and I told them, "This is your mother's final gift to our family. She made a final sacrifice to continue taking care of us, and she would want us to be happy."

I say these words and I comfort my kids, but I still struggle with this daily. It's a total mind game. So many people have been willing to help and have reached out to us and offered what they could. It's so hard to accept the idea that we can really use the assistance, and accept why we need that help.

It's also hard to allow ourselves to be happy without her. I know the eventual goal of grieving is to move beyond emptiness and loss and feel happy again, but I have been blindsided by how strange it feels to have good things come from Heidi's death. I think about Heidi every day. I miss her every day. I would gladly give back all the good we are experiencing to have Heidi back in our old lives, but that can't happen. I have to remind myself that it's okay to do these positive things, and to accept help, and it's okay to be happy.

Feelings like joy and gratitude seem out of place in my period of mourning, yet they, too, show themselves. Life creates positive moments all the time, but in the midst of grieving, it is hard to accept them, especially those that wouldn't have existed had Heidi still been living. Allowing even the tiniest amount of good into our lives feels wrong. Any positive is immediately greeted with a "How dare you!" inside my head; guilt for feeling even slightly thankful for anything we received.

When my emotional brain is done beating me up, the logical part of my brain helps me rationalize and accept my dilemma. It reminds me that no matter what emotion comes into my head, no matter what I do or how I feel, it won't bring Heidi back. Most importantly, my logical brain reminds me that Heidi would want us to be happy, as I would want for her. She wouldn't want us to wear black and grieve forever. She would want us to go on with our lives and keep living. So when I received the check from Heidi's life insurance, I knew I had to use it for our family's happiness.

Heidi always believed in building family memories. She felt it was important to take snapshots in our minds that we could hold on to forever. "Memories have longevity beyond any material item, and they can never be taken away," she would say. She was always concerned that we weren't doing enough to create memories. She would often request that we get out of town for day trips or for the weekend. These trips never had to be anything extravagant, they just needed to be time spent together. But life typically got in the way; a weekend trip was too expensive, a day trip felt like too much driving, we had too many errands to run, or the kids had too much homework; there were a million reasons not to go.

When I received Heidi's life insurance money, I made a conscious decision to use some of it to honor her wishes. I set aside some of the money to travel with the kids. We would go on the kinds of trips we had never been able to afford. Knowing the first year was going to be emotionally challenging, I didn't want us lying around the house focused on the emptiness that Heidi's death had left behind. I knew that the first year would fill us with difficult memories, such as Thanksgiving, Hanukkah, and Mother's Day. I wanted to interject positive memories to balance the negative ones. So, I came up with a deliberate strategy to help us get through that time.

I would use travel as a distraction. I figured if we had something to look forward to every couple of months, it would help us navigate and survive the year ahead. "Fake it till you make it," so to speak. Our first trip will be to Disneyland in October. And I'm planning a Caribbean cruise for spring break in March, four days in San Francisco over the Fourth of July, and a week in Maui during fall break in October 2016.

I told the kids that we will be traveling for a year and not to get used to it because we couldn't live like rich people forever.

I've also joined a gym. It's been at least twenty years since I've set foot inside a gym, and things have changed. I met my personal trainer, Aaron, who is 6'2" and bald, with a sculpted figure of less than 3 percent body fat. He looks like a gladiator ready to step into the Colosseum and do battle. Aaron is helping me discover just how out of shape I am. He introduced me to dizziness and nausea and showed me how to change my skin color without using any cosmetic products. I am in absolute disbelief that people love working out and feel incomplete without it. I am certainly not one of those people. As soon as somebody invents the "get in shape" pill, I'm going to be first in line.

I do worry that my moving forward will move me too far away from her. I hope I'm doing right by myself and by my children, and that I can be an example of how to be strong and how to heal. I wish I knew what all this is supposed to look and feel like. My whole life is now a do-over, and I hope I do a good job with this new start, with these new "positives." I don't know what the future holds; I can only continue to walk toward it and let life lead the way.

Thank you to all who have been reading and commenting. This public forum has allowed me to recognize the emotions and feelings that have become present, to write about them and release them so I don't have to hold them inside and let them fester. I am finding that my need to post is stretching out, and I think that's a good thing. I will just have to live each day and see what happens.

Chapter 15

An Empty Drawer

October 1, 2015, 8:10 p.m. (Day 31)

What a difference a day makes. What a difference a moment makes. Tonight, I'm sad and lonely. As I've stated before, this journey changes by the moment. Yesterday was good; tonight, not so much.

I went to work today and was productive. The day moved forward in normal time and all appeared to be going normally. Then I got home.

Judy told me she had started to go through the drawers in the dresser, as I had requested. She had one drawer done, and that was all she could handle. When I saw the empty drawer, it was hard to take in. Empty. Such a fitting word.

Soon there will be more empty drawers, and then we will remove Heidi's clothes from the closet, and that too will be empty. I know we need to do this, but how the hell do you manage this? Perhaps I am being overly dramatic. I thought this task wouldn't be so bad and that I was ready for it. Perhaps I am not?

I returned to stare into the empty drawer. A drawer with so much history connected to it. A drawer that served Judy and Ira, Heidi's parents, and then went on to serve Heidi and me. What stories would this drawer tell; what service this drawer has provided over the decades.

I'd never really looked at it before. My eyes traveled the lines of its perimeter. It hides behind two cabinet doors that swing open, revealing two other drawers that together make up the dresser. Furniture isn't made like this anymore: the wood is solid, and the strength of its construction shines through. I grabbed the handles and pulled, revealing the empty interior. I focused on every grain of wood, every tongue and groove holding it in place. Only memories of what once filled those spaces exist now. . . .

The late afternoon sun shines through the bedroom windows, creating spotlights that illuminate the walls. The sounds of three young children arguing over nothing and doing homework can be heard across the house in the distance. A woman enters, carrying a large plastic basket filled with clothing fresh from the dryer, her long, shiny black hair brushing against her shoulders. The aroma of fabric softener wafts from the basket. She tosses the newly washed clothes onto the bed and, one-by-one, folds and organizes them into groups that will be distributed later.

She takes a turtleneck from the pile and places it facedown; her hands move across it, smoothing it as she goes, pulling it tight to the sides before folding it. She places it aside and repeats the process several times, stacking the turtlenecks without giving any thought to her actions. In a family of five, so many tasks become automatic.

With the turtlenecks in hand, she turns and pulls the handles to open the heavy drawer with the balance and finesse that only a mother can produce. Inside the drawer, the turtlenecks are arranged by color—a stack of white next to a stack of black. White and black match just about everything she wears, so it makes sense to be well equipped in these colors.

The turtlenecks are restocked, filling the entire drawer. They aren't fancy—100 percent cotton and thick to the touch. There are so many because even in the Arizona heat, she's always cold. Using both hands, she gives the drawer a good push. It skips a little along its tracks as it retires back into the dresser.

In the evening, she returns, opens the drawer, and pulls out a black turtleneck. After a quick change and a short walk to the closet, she grabs a lightweight red velour jacket, her favorite. She puts it on over her turtleneck and stops for a glance in front of the full-length mirror. The zipper goes up, then back down, then up again, finally resting somewhere in the middle. With a satisfied look on her face, she walks out of the room.

My head turned away from the drawer for a moment as if to watch her leave. I noticed the red velour jacket hanging in the closet, where it will remain. The turtlenecks filled a black plastic trash bag in the corner. I turned back and stared into the empty drawer. I heard myself release a heavy sigh before I pushed the drawer closed and left the room.

This weekend, but not tonight, I will continue to empty the dresser.

Chapter 16

The Not-So-Happiest Place on Earth

October 6, 2015, 7:36 p.m. (Day 36)

What does getting better look like? I don't know exactly, but I think I might be starting to see it.

Last week was the first one that actually felt like a week and not a year. I'm beginning to find my groove at work, and I'm finding that the ideas for things to write about are becoming fewer and further apart. That being said, I would not consider myself to be fantastic by any means. If the right moment hits me, I still break down. I also still cannot shake this paradox of positive and negative sharing the same space.

This morning I went to the bank and deposited the life insurance check. As I was sitting there with the banker, I couldn't ignore my inner conflict. The check I deposited allowed me to work on my own health. It removed some of the financial burden that Heidi and I lived under our entire time together. It allowed me to provide for my children in ways that I couldn't in the past. Yet, this check was only here because of Heidi's passing. I would trade every penny for the ability to go back and hear the words "cancer-free."

Although I feel like I am healing, it's still merely five weeks since Heidi's death. I wonder how I can find anything to be happy about. Yet

I can. The kids and I leave for Disneyland this weekend, and I'm really looking forward to it.

What does grief look like? Does it have to look like darkness that won't go away? Does it have to look like being in a corner curled up in a ball? The truth is, I have no idea what grief is supposed to look like. I've never walked this path before. I don't know how I am supposed to be or what I'm supposed to feel. I can only acknowledge what shows up, and for now what is showing up seems to be okay on average.

October 7, 2015, 11:11 p.m. (Day 37)

When the kids go to bed and the house gets very quiet, this is when I find myself in the reality of my situation. Tonight, I was looking over some of Heidi's pictures on her Facebook page and came across the one with her and Max at the airport in July on our way to Portland to spend time with her brother and his family. This was a happy day. It was Max's first airplane ride. What a gift it was that Heidi was there to share it with him. There is something piercing about this photo. I found myself not being able to look away. I zoomed in on her face, and it felt like she was looking right at me. She looks tired but happy. Max looks happy. It saddens me to look at it. It tells the tale of a mother's love for her son, for her family. Who knew at the time that this would be our last vacation together as a whole family? That in just a little over one month Heidi would be gone forever? I look at this picture, and all I want to say is that this is not right! Heidi was forty-seven years old; she had a whole life ahead of her. She had Jack's and Max's bar mitzvahs to attend. Graduations to attend. She needed to see what would become of her children as they grew into adults. She would have had grandchildren to spoil and enjoy. She had so much left to do.

When Heidi was initially diagnosed, the doctor told her that this was not genetic or inherited. She said that this was just "bad luck cancer." Bad luck cancer? This is unbelievable to me. If there was anyone on this earth that did not deserve "bad luck cancer" it was Heidi. Heidi was a woman who gave to others tirelessly. Heidi brightened people's day, every day. Heidi was anything but deserving of "bad luck cancer." I just don't understand.

October 8, 2015, 9:15 a.m. (Day 38)

The tasks of daily living are so tough. I am prepping the family to go on this trip to Disneyland this weekend, and I am finding it extremely challenging. In my past life, Heidi would get the family ready to go. She would get out her many lists and get everything done, one task at a time. When we traveled, she would usually start preparing a week in advance. She would fill little bottles with shampoo and conditioner. She would gather up the diabetes supplies for Jack, which was like packing for another child altogether. She would get outfits for the kids and always two or three extras. She would get her pharmacy ready to go: she had an on-the-go remedy for anything you could imagine. She did all this like a well-oiled machine. Everything would be ready the night before we left; we were golden.

For this trip, I don't have Heidi, the queen of organization. This task is left to me. I fear that it's almost more than I can handle. There is so much to take care of. Last night, as I started to pack with the kids (note that I just started, and we leave in two days), I noticed the underwear Max had at the ready looked a little small. I had him try it on, and I saw his legs nearly turn blue from lack of circulation. Yup—he needed the next size up. Thank goodness Target has late hours. 9:10 at night, and I was off to Target for some underwear.

When we got home, I had him go get a pair of long pants, just in case it got cold. He didn't have any that fit. Keeping my kids properly clothed will be one more task I will have to master.

Also, last night Madeline came to me and asked if she could have some friends over for a sleepover next week when we get back. Why do teenage girls always want the sleepover? I asked what she had in mind and how many girls she was thinking about. She counted on her fingers and answered confidently—nine! I almost had a heart attack on the spot. Sleepovers freak me out. What am I supposed to do with nine teenage girls? What do I feed them? What do I have them do? Where do they sleep? OMG! I wanted to say no, but when I look into her eyes, I am such a sucker. She's a daddy's girl, and I am her daddy; what can I say? So it appears that I will be having a gaggle of girls over next weekend.

I don't know how Heidi always kept this family going for whatever we needed. Now this task has fallen on me. How do I do this and work? How do I manage all that's weighing on me without blowing up? Work needs me full-time, and my family needs me full-time. I don't know how to be everything to everybody. There are only so many hours in the day, and I don't know how to allocate my time to be most efficient when my tasks of work and fatherhood lie in conflict with one another. It is such a struggle to be the best at both. I am so afraid of screwing up one or both. I hope I rise to the task, find this balance to manage all who need me, and do a good job.

October 9, 2015, 11:00 p.m. (Day 39)

Tomorrow we go to the Happiest Place on Earth, yet I can't help but be a little apprehensive. Disneyland was always a big deal for our family. It was one of Heidi's favorite places. We have so much history there. We have the place where, at age three, Jack had a tantrum, and the other place where Jack had a tantrum, and the other place where Jack had a tantrum. We have Madeline's throw-up table in California Adventure, and right off Main Street we have Jack's garbage can where he lost his Disney magnet, and we had to ask an employee to dig through the trash and find it for us. We have our tradition of taking the train to Toontown and riding It's a Small World before we can do anything else. We have so many memories there. What we don't have is another chance to share it all with Heidi.

I am worried that this loss will be in control, that it will have a hold on me, and that it won't let go. I am worried that everywhere I go, I will see Heidi; that this fun time will be more than I can bear.

I know it's important to keep going and to make new memories. I just fear that tomorrow will be like walking down a familiar road but not recognizing any of the landmarks.

This is crazy, I mean it's Disneyland, for cryin' out loud! It's Mickey and Minnie, it's Splash Mountain and the Matterhorn. It's California Screamin' and Toy Story. There is so much to do and to experience; there is so much fun. I just can't seem to shake this underlying layer of concern.

When I close my eyes, I see her everywhere at this park. I have flashbacks that are like still photos in my mind. A snapshot of us in a line to get her favorite Disney meal, the beef and chicken skewers in Adventureland. A snapshot of us on the Jungle Cruise hearing the same jokes we've heard for years. A snapshot standing in our spot in front of the photo store on Main Street, waiting for the fireworks to start. How will I handle tomorrow when all I have are snapshots?

Tomorrow will be another first for me and the kids, another test of our ability to persevere through this emotional roller coaster that we didn't stand in line to ride.

October 10, 2015, 11:14 p.m. (Day 40)

Today marked the start of our family's fifth trip to Disneyland. During our previous trips, as soon as we arrived on the street that housed our hotel, an overwhelming sense of familiarity and comfort came over me. It always felt like a home away from home.

Today was different. For the first time, I didn't feel the excitement of being here. Everything changed. Everything about today was sad and hard to take. I couldn't summon a smile.

Thank goodness the boys didn't share my emotional experience. They were giddy with excitement. Except for a stray comment here and there about how strange it was to be here without Mom, they had a good day. It was not so easy for Madeline. She was a little cranky and impatient with the boys' crazy behavior. She said countless times that the boys were driving her mad. I sensed it was not only the boys affecting her. I knew it was the same struggle I was facing, and after a talk later this evening, my concern was confirmed.

This is not an easy trip. I've been fearful that maybe I made the wrong decision to bring us here. Maybe I exaggerated my own strength and my family's slow-growing emotional stability. Nonetheless, we are here.

We arrived at the park today in the midafternoon. Upon entering, we went to City Hall and found out what the new guest assistance opportunities were for Type 1 diabetics. In the past, we had been able to jump all the lines and go straight to the front. The new policy involved timed entries that required more planning. With the changes, the kids decided they didn't want to repeat our tradition of going on It's a Small World first. I guess that tradition will die with Heidi. I understood this decision, but it saddened me.

As we began to ride attractions, we were hit in the face every time a ride worker asked us "How many in your party?" It affected all of us to say "Four." Nothing at Disneyland was joyful for me. I wanted more than anything to smile but couldn't muster the energy to do so. Nothing felt real. We're a broken family, and I feel I have to fix us.

I have to live this trip through my boys' eyes tomorrow. I have to feel the excitement, the happiness. I have to help my daughter feel this, too. I have to keep this family alive.

October 11, 2015, 7:24 a.m. (Day 41)

It's another day, and I am no better than yesterday. How much can a person cry?

The boys are starting to wake up, and we will soon get ready to go downstairs and feed our faces with a buffet of eggs, waffles, bacon or sausage, and Frosted Flakes. This is a moment the boys have been looking forward to. In the past, Heidi never could make it down to join us; it took an entire morning for her to pull herself together and get ready to face a day. We'd always take a plate back to her. Eggs, bacon, a bagel, and some pancakes or French toast, depending on what was available. Today there will be no food to go. When we are done, we will be done.

This is so hard, and I miss her so much. It is unbearable.

October 11, 2015, 11:37 a.m. (Day 41)

I am waiting for the kids to get off Goofy's Flight School. The day is getting better, but I am forcing that—mind over matter. I've never had to struggle so much to have a good time, especially at a place like Disneyland.

It's mind-boggling how happiness is a moment-to-moment struggle. I look around this place, and I can tell you where the bathrooms are all located, where every kind of restaurant is, and how to navigate the map to make the most efficient path for riding attractions. With all this familiarity, I still feel like I am lost in a foreign country without a guide.

October 11, 2015, 11:31 p.m. (Day 41)

As today progressed, I felt the Disney Magic beginning to cut through the clouds of my emotions. I started to feel a real breakthrough. I began to accept our new family picture pose with only the four of us—me in the back and the three kids in the front. I do believe I even started to enjoy myself having fun with the kids. It turned into a typical Disney day, overspending on candy and food, walking 9.25 miles, according to Max's Fitbit, and enjoying the Happiest Place on Earth, despite the ungodly 97-degree weather. The late-night agenda was to stay and watch the spectacular new fireworks display that was created just for Disney's Diamond Celebration.

The park was packed shoulder to shoulder and elbow to elbow with people. As the Main Street lights dimmed and the music began to play, the sky lit up with loud explosions of light and sound. There were light projections on all the Main Street buildings as well as on the castle. It truly was spectacular. As the show continued, I began to find myself distancing from the show with every bang. I became overwhelmed with emotion and began to cry. Every flash or boom caused another tear. This went on for most of the show.

There must have been tens of thousands of people watching this show in awe. I felt sure that I was the only one draped in sadness and crying uncontrollably.

Your brain does this to you, it tells you you're the only one, you're completely alone, and yet, of course, that crowd was full of people who were dealing with their own losses, their own heartbreak. Statistically speaking, it was impossible that I was the only one in pain. Surely, there were kids somewhere in that crowd who were facing a terminal illness and had been brought to Disney to fulfill some final request. There had to be people who had lost significant others as well. There were undoubtedly hundreds of people there who were in a similar spot to me, but in that moment I was convinced I was the only one. It's a mind lie, which is part of the grief process. You're already in horrible pain, and then your brain tells you you're all alone, there's no one else grieving, everybody else is happy. There's no one who understands. Your brain creates perceptions that make what you're already facing even more painful.

Heidi and I absolutely loved the fireworks. We would stay to watch them every night we could. We even had a viewing spot that we returned to year after year, right in front of the photo shop on Main Street where they rope off the street to allow cross traffic. In our opinion, that was the best fireworks viewing spot in the park. It has an unhindered view of the castle, which is at the center of the action. Perhaps Heidi was there watching this show with me one last time. Maybe that's why I became overwhelmed; I would like to think so. Maybe she is still enjoying the incredible fireworks display that Disney puts on. Just maybe?

October 12, 2015, 3:47 p.m. (Day 42)

I cannot seem to shake the blues. I am still in the Happiest Place on Earth, and all I can seem to muster is a so-so. I am going through the motions. I fear that for me, Disneyland has lost the magic. Maybe it was too soon. Maybe it was the wrong place. Maybe time will tell me how this trip really was. I look around, and I see families having a good time. Smiles are everywhere. Kids are running because walking is just too slow. What is wrong with me?

Will I ever be able to come back here, or is this the end of Disneyland for me? I need to be able to laugh again; I need to be able to enjoy life. How does one do that? How does one reintroduce joy? What does joy look like?

Today I don't know the answers. I hope over time these answers will show themselves. Moving forward is such an overwhelming task. It requires all I have to give. It requires tremendous focus, and if I slip, even just the slightest bit, I fall down a tremendous hole and have to inch my way back to where I already was.

So I keep plugging along, I keep acting, and I keep hoping my kids don't find out who is behind the curtain.

October 13, 2015, 11:38 p.m. (Day 43)

I finally had a good day. Ironically, it was our last day. I guess if you wake up every day and tell yourself today will be a better day, eventually you have one. Today was a better day.

Grief is a tug-of-war. For three of my four vacation days, grief had the upper hand. Today, I pulled the rope. It was finally nice to enjoy a Disney day with my kids. It was like old times.

I had been thinking about finding the perfect Disney rock for Heidi. In Jewish tradition when visiting the grave of a loved one who has passed, it is customary to bring a rock and place it on their gravestone. I wanted to do this for Heidi since this place had such meaning for her. I've been looking for a rock for three days. Would you believe that there are practically no small rocks in either Disneyland or California Adventure? There are plenty of planters and lots of pretty landscaping, but no rocks. I had pretty much decided that the only rocks I would be able to get were the polished stones you buy by the bag for $6.00. Then the kids and I went on Big Thunder Mountain today for our last time. Note that this was our third time this trip. Also note that we all had been looking for rocks for the last three days and hadn't been able to find any. Suddenly, today, I looked at the ground and discovered that this entire ride is covered in small rocks. They were everywhere! How did I miss this the other two times? I felt like I hit the Heidi jackpot. I gathered up rocks for me and the kids, and it was finally mission accomplished. Not surprisingly, Big Thunder Mountain was Heidi's favorite ride in the park.

The tradition states that when you place a rock on a loved one's headstone, the rock touches the ground, and the ground touches the casket, which embraces the body. Therefore, the rock is like giving a loved one a hug. When I get back, I will go see Heidi for the first time. I'll place the rock I brought home from Disneyland at Heidi's gravesite, and I will give her a hug.

I realize that with the transition into October, the fog has lifted, and its numbness has loosened its hold. As I emerge and reenter the world I checked out of, it looks and feels different. I am no longer under the fog's protection; I have to face life head on, and it terrifies me.

As I enter the next phase of the healing process and the tasks of living begin to stack up, I've become preoccupied and overwhelmed with a fear of failure and feelings of inadequacy. I doubt my stamina to keep pace. There are so many aspects of my past life with Heidi that I have taken for granted. The amount of effort needed to keep a family of five—now four—running, has opened my eyes and made me appreciate the job Heidi did every day. The refrigerator and pantry need to be stocked with after-school snacks for the kids. Dinners need to be planned and prepared. Groceries have to be bought, at different stores, because one store doesn't have everything we need. Laundry—oh, so much laundry—has to be done multiple times a week. These are just the basics. Additionally, the kids need to be picked up from two different schools at the same time. There are doctor, dentist, and orthodontist appointments to schedule and shuttle the kids to. There are tennis, flag football, and basketball practices. The list goes on and on. Each task is filling me with self-doubt. How can one person possibly stay on top of it all?

The challenges at home are compounded by the demands placed upon me at work. I am not just an office worker who arrives in the morning, punches in, sits at a desk for eight hours pushing paper and then goes home. I am a partner in a small insurance agency, where no one is expendable. Like members of a rock band, everyone is a soloist.

My time and attention are in high demand; my kids need me at home, and my partners and employees need me at work. I wonder how I will be able to show up for everyone. I wonder where the energy will come from. I fear I won't be able to divide my time effectively and that I will fail as both a father and a company partner.

And I'm still grieving.

Yet as I look at the faces of my children, I notice that, for the most part, the magic of Disney has worked for them. Somehow they have managed to have a good time and show genuine signs of excitement and joy. They are not weighed down by memories as I've been. Though I worried that they would somehow tap into my emotional state and be dragged down.

I'm not the great actor I would like to think I am, and if confronted, I knew I wouldn't be able to lie to my children. In order to shield my children from what I was experiencing, I dug deep, put on a facade, and went undercover. I became someone I wasn't. I utilized all my energy to quell my emotions and appear to be having a good time, as my children were. When they looked at me, I was smiling; when they looked away, I frowned. I was living two different experiences, one for them and one for myself. I had to be present for my children. The responsibility of parenthood never felt so great.

It's hard to be fraudulent, especially to the ones you love, but it was my love for them that drove me. My desire to keep them safe and emotionally protected gave me the strength to appear differently. Consequently—and interestingly—the exercise of pretending to be happy for them ultimately allowed a little bit of happiness for me. It takes a lot of work to be happy. Grief is still in charge, and it doesn't seem to be letting go anytime soon.

The Disneyland experience has made me question how I will handle future trips with just the four of us. This first one had been so draining, and being the only adult had added layers of pressure and responsibility.

Being at the Happiest Place on Earth and not feeling happy made me question whether I would ever feel normal again. How hard will I have to look, how long will I have to wait to find joy in my life again?

The truth is, there is no secret, no spell that wears off. Tinkerbell can't fly over us, wave her magic wand or sprinkle fairy dust on us and make everything better. It takes work. I have to want to be happy again; I have to force it. I have to wake up every day and will myself to be better. It will be hard, and there will be plenty of obstacles in the way. I will be swimming against the current, but in order to succeed I have to just keep swimming. For me, it is about tomorrow. I will speak aloud the words "Tomorrow will be another day; tomorrow might be different." Finding happiness again will just take time.

Chapter 17

Backward Isn't Really Backward

October 14, 2015, 9:27 p.m. (Day 44)

I'm a wreck. Prior to our trip, I really felt good. I was emotionally strong and moving forward beyond Heidi's passing remarkably well, maybe even too well. I guess this is the thing about grief. It comes and goes like the rising tide.

This trip has set me back emotionally by a month. It feels like it was only two weeks ago, and not six, that she died. Although the days don't seem like years, the emotions of the days are certainly at the forefront. I am walking around in a daze. I can't seem to find myself. This is all too familiar. Maybe this is just how it goes. On the one hand, I am glad to feel grief because I was afraid of losing touch with just how difficult this is. On the other hand, grief really hurts. If this is what it will be like, and it has only been a month and a half, how am I supposed to deal with this for the next month, or months, or years?

Before our trip to Disneyland, I felt strong and confident, even if somewhat worried. I felt in control of my emotions and not that my emotions had control of me. Boy was I wrong. I feel like I got hit by a Mack truck and thrown back a mile. Now I have to get up, dust myself off, and walk back to where I was before. Is my life going to be a big circle? How do I move forward and stay forward? I have no idea.

October 14, 2015, 9:41 p.m. (Day 44)

I just wrote a post about my emotional state. After posting, I wanted to call my mother, hear an encouraging word or two, and tell her about my trip. When I dialed her number, it rang and rang and rang, but nobody was picking up. Not even the answering machine. Strange. Then it hit me, hard: this is what my children are going through every day. How unfair! They are experiencing the agony of wanting to talk their mom but not having her available. This makes me so sad for my kids; I don't know how to make this better for them. Then my phone rang. It was my mom calling back. I will call her back now, something my kids will never be able to do with their mom.

October 16, 2015, 9:10 p.m. (Day 46)

Since Heidi's passing there have been endless tasks that needed to be done. I had to change the cable out of her name and put it into mine. I had to remove her from the health insurance policy and cancel her credit cards. These tasks are not difficult, and they're necessary and part of moving forward. What makes them hard is the people at the call center on the other side of the phone. With every call I have to announce the reason for the call and the reason for the change.

"I need to take care of this because on August 31 Heidi passed away," I say.

What comes next is always the worst: "Oh, my sincere condolences."

But the condolences are anything but sincere. The people I am speaking with are corporately trained to respond, and it's like fingernails on a chalkboard. It is an awkward moment. I don't know them, they don't know me, and they surely did not know Heidi. I know they have to say that, and they are in a catch-22 because if they don't say anything, the customer might think they are rude.

The problem is that I am moving forward, which is not to be confused with "healed" or "better." Every time I hear a fresh "I'm so sorry for your loss," or a "My sincere condolences," it drags me down. With those words, I have to relive this over and over. It's a tough position because I don't want to sound heartless or rude, but it's hard to move forward when you're continuously being driven back.

This happens with clients and friends as well. Although not as annoying, it has a similar effect, though I feel that at least it is more sincere and heartfelt than it is from a complete stranger. I can at least appreciate the place it's coming from. However, the result is still the same. It keeps the emotions fresh. I think what happens is when I run into someone or speak with someone for the first time, for them it is the first time, but for me it's a month and half later. I don't want to sound cold, but this whole process is exhausting. It's a moment-by-moment struggle to stay in the world and be a part of it. There are so many firsts I have to deal with and to adjust to; it's hard to manage and adjust to the firsts of others.

Recently, I went to a deli Heidi and I had frequented, and sitting at one of the tables was the owner. I hadn't seen her in a while, but the last time I saw her I informed her that Heidi was at home battling cancer. She told me I was not allowed to pay for the sandwiches I was picking up. Feeding me was the very least she could do to help. I barely knew this woman, yet she showed me great kindness and compassion. Seeing her there again, I knew I would face another one of those awkward grief moments. Her husband, who also works in the restaurant and who I see more often, must have told her about Heidi's passing, because when she approached, she asked me how long it had been since I lost my wife. She asked me how the kids and I were doing. In between her questions, she repeated the phrase "God bless you."

In my head, I said, "Lady, I just want to eat my sandwich," but of course, that is not how these encounters go.

I answered her questions, and once again she said, "Let me get you some sandwiches to take home to the kids. God bless you." I said that was a truly kind gesture, but I didn't need to take sandwiches. "I am going to at least bring you over a cannoli," she insisted. She had to do something.

I was moved by her kindness, of course, and yet it reminded me that I still faced daily trials when the grief inside me fought to come out. When I left, I fought back tears, and my day had changed.

Chapter 18

Acting Out

October 21, 2015, 11:34 p.m. (Day 51)

I don't know what to do. My little guy Max and I just got into a tiff. Around 9:30 Max put on a TV show and fell asleep in my bed. After a little while, I woke him up and helped him back to his bed. I've done this hundreds of times, and moving him has always been easy. In fact, so many times in the past when I moved him, he'd still be semi-asleep and do very funny things that little kids do when they are sleep walking. He'd go the wrong way, away from his room. He would get into his bed and put his head where his feet should go, and sometimes he wouldn't even make it to his bed; he would just bend over, half in and half out, and fall asleep right there. He was so entertaining that Jack and I would call this transition "The Max Show." Tonight there was no show.

Lately, things with Max have changed. He's been complaining that his bed is too hard or the room is too cold or too hot, when nothing is physically different. He seems to be having trouble sleeping in his bed. The other night, he asked Jack to switch beds with him, and Jack did. This was not such a good move for Max. At 3:00 a.m. when I went to check Jack's blood glucose numbers, I didn't realize they had switched beds, and I poked Max and squeezed out Max's blood to test. Of course, he woke up, and the look on his face was priceless. Oops!

Tonight I ran out of patience. Shortly after I moved him to his own bed, he came back out of his room to tell me he couldn't sleep. I didn't want to deal. I yelled a little bit and told him to go back to bed, to sleep on the floor, or whatever! He said he couldn't sleep in his bed and he needed his sleep to function. He told me he wouldn't be able to go to school ever again because he wouldn't have any sleep, and school is too hard without sleep. He also threw in several cuss words, told me I was a bad dad and that I didn't care about him. After a time, he came back into my room without the attitude and said I should take him to a doctor to see why he isn't sleeping.

It's hard to stay mad at little Max. When we were able to talk calmly, I told him the problem isn't his bed. I told him his bed has been fine for years. I told him he has only had issues with his bed since Mom died. Then it hit me: maybe this is the problem. I asked him directly if that might be part of the problem, and he shook his head no. I have to believe this is related. I just have no clue how to get through to him and to dig for the real reasons for the sleeping problem.

"Mother" is a comfort word, especially when you're ten years old. Max is the ultimate mama's boy, and Heidi was a powerful nurturing presence in his life. She was a down comforter on a cold night, a warm cup of hot chocolate in front of a fire. To Max, she was that and more. Losing her shocked his system; he needs daily reassurance, hugs, and love. He looked to me to fill that space. The night of Heidi's passing, he stayed in my bed because being close to me replaced some of the comfort that had been taken away. I didn't mind because I knew it was helping him put his shattered world back together. I knew this couldn't go on indefinitely. Eventually, he would need to make his way back to his room and start sleeping on his own again.

I was cautious not to push him out, but checked in with him: "What do you think about sleeping in your room again?" I asked.

He looked off, pondering my question. "Maybe in a few nights I could try it," he said.

How do you get a ten-year-old to act like an adult and express feelings and work through loss issues? This is a challenge. I want to help him, but I don't know how. There are clearly issues he is suffering with.

Last week we started grief counseling. It's group therapy where we're all divided into peer groups. I hope this will help Max and the other kids; perhaps it will even help me. Tonight I gave in. Max is now sleeping in my bed.

October 22, 2015, 8:02 a.m. (Day 52)

The game has changed. My little argument with Max last night made me really reflect. Before Heidi's death, getting angry with my kids was normal and natural. I see now that getting angry was a privilege. It was easy to do, and bad behavior was obvious. Now everything is different. Bad behavior might not be bad behavior.

I remember last week in Disneyland when Madeline was acting out, and suddenly she was pinching her brothers again. This behavior was not Madeline being short-tempered; I am convinced this was Madeline coping with the emotionally draining fact that we were at Disneyland without Mom. Last night, when Max couldn't sleep, this was not Max suddenly determining that his bed was too hard; this was Max dealing with the realization that he no longer has the comfort of his mother, which he needs more than anything.

I can no longer be a surface father; those days are over. I have to look at every situation and determine what is behind it. Now don't get me wrong, I'm sure there will be times when my kids will just be my kids and be behaving terribly. At those times, they'll deserve a good scolding and some discipline. However, everything is different now. Red might not be red, and blue might not be blue. It will be my challenge to see beyond the surface and determine what is in front of me. The freedom I had before to be self-focused has been taken away. I have to be mother and father. I have to be family therapist and doctor; captain of this ship without a first mate. I have to take any blinders off and see my new world through widened eyes. Nothing might be as it appears.

Chapter 19

The Big Blue Cart

October 24, 2015, 4:09 p.m. (Day 54)

For eight weeks—a full three weeks since I tackled emptying Heidi's dresser—I have been looking at a closet filled with Heidi's clothing. She had so many clothes. She had old clothes and new clothes, skinny clothes and not-so-skinny clothes. She had summer clothes and winter clothes. She even still had maternity clothes. I guess one could say that Heidi really liked clothes.

There is no door on my closet, and it is completely visible from the bed and the chairs in my bedroom. Everywhere I looked, there were her clothes. Today was the day I went through the closet. It's a hard thing to do. Every time I do something like this, I can't help but feel like I am slowly erasing her. With every armload I took to the car, it felt like I was cutting one more line of her story. I know this has to be done, but logic doesn't make it any easier.

Judy and I loaded up almost the entire van and drove it to Goodwill. Hopefully, someone else will gain joy from those clothes. Once we were parked, the attendant came up with his big blue cart and asked me, "How are you doing?" There is that normal question at an abnormal moment, once again. How do you answer that? "Oh, I am fine; I just came here to give you my wife."

Of course, I didn't say that. I answered the same way I always do when people ask me that: "I'm fine."

We loaded that blue cart to the breaking point. The amount of clothing that fit inside truly made me wonder if Heidi knew there were only seven days in a week. Once the cart was full, the attendant pushed it around my car and over to the double doors.

Here I am again, holding out my hand, but I'm not at Heidi's funeral; I'm in front of a Goodwill donation center. And it's not Heidi's casket I'm watching drop beneath the earth. It's a nondescript, large blue plastic cart, filled with Heidi's clothing. The clothing inside touched her in life as she wore it against her skin. The colors and styles defined her personality, and the quantity and sizes illustrated the love/hate relationship she had with clothing.

After Heidi's passing, her clothing remained a symbol of her presence, and thus, paradoxically, of her absence as well. Staring into her closet full of clothes, I saw beyond the hangers; I saw her grabbing a shirt, putting it on, then taking it off and grabbing another. I heard her asking me which blouse looked better with what necklace. I saw her step into the black sheepskin Ugg boots she wore for years that never went out of style.

Emptying the closet, I peeled away the layers of my wife one by one. I touched the dress pants and blouse she wore to Madeline's bat mitzvah. It took her three trips to the mall to find them, but they were the perfect outfit that overcame the ugliness of cancer and allowed her to feel the joy of the celebration. I unclipped from the hangers the pairs of jeans she wore on the weekends as we walked the aisles of the supermarket gathering groceries for the week. I filled up my arms with fuzzy socks and maternity T-shirts she used as sleep shirts that kept her warm every night; they were big and comfy and each shirt had its share of holes, exposing a glimpse of her arms or back. Everything I touched had a memory connected to it. For years, Heidi and I took things to Goodwill. We released ourselves of things we no longer needed. With this trip, I was making a run loaded with things I needed, but couldn't keep. What I loaded into that cart was not just material, buttons and zippers; inside that cart was Heidi.

I couldn't escape the emotional parallels as I watched each revolution of the wheels move the cart farther away from me. This time Heidi wasn't surrounded by those who loved her; she was pushed by an unwitting participant, a worker just doing his job, oblivious to the "second funeral" taking place.

The attendant, the cart, and Heidi disappeared. I took a breath in that space before walking away and breathing once again into my new life.

October 25, 2015, 7:45 a.m. (Day 55)

People say that loved ones visit you in dreams after they have passed. Well, it has been almost two months, and the only dream I'd had with Heidi in it was the one I had shortly after she died. That was a terrible dream.

Last night, that changed. In the middle of whatever dream I was having, I had an image take over. It was Heidi lying next to me in my bed. I was looking at her, and she was looking at me. I had my hand on her cheek, and I could feel her skin against mine. It was so vivid and real. I remember in my dream I was whimpering and crying out loud because I couldn't believe she was really here next to me. We were just looking into each other's faces. She had a smile on hers, as she looked into my eyes, as if to reassure me that everything was okay.

It was very short, and then my dream moved on to other things. It was great to be with her again, even if only in my dream for a few seconds.

I miss her terribly, every day!

October 27, 2015, 11:22 p.m. (Day 57)

Heidi juggled kids, laundry, homework, activities, grocery shopping, clothing shopping, dinners, and Jack's diabetes. I don't know how she did it. Maybe the female DNA is uniquely made up to handle all this juggling. Maybe it was Heidi's Type-A personality that qualified her to manage all the needs of our family.

Now it has become my turn to juggle everything that has fallen on my shoulders. With every ball I add comes more chaos. Thank God for Judy. Without her, I don't know what I would do.

There are so many things I wished I had paid more attention to, like how to back up an iPhone, how to set up an Evite for Madeline's upcoming party for her fourteenth birthday, or how to adjust Jack's insulin settings on his pump. Everything has become on-the-job training.

In addition, I still have the things I always did, like going to work, taking the car in for an oil change, paying the bills, and balancing the checking account. It's overwhelming.

I think the pressure of all this has finally gotten to me. The last two nights, I've been stressed when I arrived home, and short-tempered and impatient with the kids. I try so hard to stay even-keeled, but sometimes I just can't. Of course, now if I get cranky or a little loud with the kids, I feel guilty. The last thing I want to do is bring more stress into this environment or fight with my children. Family is precious, and I don't want to waste time arguing and yelling.

Life is different now. Things are not what they were. There may be no tomorrow. If there is no tomorrow, how do I want to spend today? Do I spend it yelling? Do I spend it arguing? I truly do not want to.

What matters? What is important? Life has become a constant check and balance.

Chapter 20

Blindsided by Anger

October 29, 2015, 9:07 a.m. (Day 59)

Today started out like any other day post-Heidi. I woke up, got the kids up, got myself ready, and got the two oldest off to school. After I dropped them, it was time to get the little one to his school. This is nothing unique; this is what I do every day now, managing tasks and managing kids. But as I drove Max to school, I couldn't stop the tears. Everything new that I'm managing is because I have lost my wife, my best friend, my life partner, my soulmate.

This loss is not just about symbols: an empty closet, a large king-size bed. It's about losing a part of my essence forever. It's about going on with only half of me left. It's challenging to complete every day with some sort of positivity. It's a loss of sharing, of companionship.

It's not easy to find that right person. People can search their entire lives and never find them. I was lucky enough not only to find that person, but to have been chosen by her as well. I was truly blessed. We didn't have an abundance of money, and ultimately we were unable to hold on to the dream house we built. What we did have was not something that could be bought or paid for, but it could be taken anywhere: what we had was love. We had a perfect gift—a perfect family with three perfect children. I didn't need anything else.

It's hard to face the fact, day in and day out, that my perfect little life has been taken away from me. Cancer has robbed me and my children of one of the greatest human beings that ever walked this earth. Cancer sucks. I hate cancer!

October 30, 2015, 10:56 p.m. (Day 60)

Last night was our second night of family peer grief counseling. In my group, a question was asked in the spirit of Halloween: "What are you afraid of?" We went around the room, and people shared different things. While they were speaking, I was thinking, "What am I afraid of?" I gave this some thought, and then it came to me, hard and clear. I'm afraid that something might happen to me like it happened to Heidi. I'm afraid that a health issue might put my life in jeopardy or kill me. If something like that happened, what would happen to my children? I am their plan A and their plan B.

Sure, I can have a trust and will drawn up. I can make contingency plans, but that isn't me raising them. Those actions wouldn't stop our family from breaking further. I am all they have. This is now my deepest fear. It's something I never had to think about before. Because of this fear, I have joined a gym and invested in a personal trainer to help guide me to better health. And for the first time in my life, I ordered salmon at the restaurant tonight. I will do everything in my power to reduce stress in my life, whether at work or at home. I have to do everything I can to stack the odds in my favor to be around to raise and take care of my kids. They are the most important thing in my world now.

November 1, 2015, 8:02 a.m. (Day 62)

Halloween has come and gone. Madeline dressed up as Tigger, Jack was Doc Brown from *Back to the Future*, and Max was a pistol-wielding skull commando—don't ask. This year was different: I was officially kicked out of Halloween. Madeline went trick-or-treating with a group of friends from her old school and then slept over, while Jack and Max and their friends decided they no longer needed the accompaniment of adults to get through trick-or-treating. I was booted.

This didn't entirely feel like a bad idea; not having to walk the neighborhood wasn't so terrible. My plan was the same as it has been for the last several years—to go over to our friends' house, have dinner, and manage Halloween. I was looking forward to it, even without my trick-or-treat participation. It would be a nice grown-up night with good friends.

I am increasingly finding myself looking forward to experiences, yet I can't truly enjoy them. My couple friends never make me feel like a third wheel, but I can't escape the feelings of being one. It's hard to be in groups without my "plus one." I can show up, but I'm challenged to sit back and enjoy the moment.

My life is all on the surface because I seem to have no depth. Every day is just going through the motions, putting on my "everything is all right" mask. I am a guest in my own life.

November 1, 2015, 12:08 p.m. (Day 62)

I visited Heidi's gravesite for the first time since we laid her to rest. It has taken me more than two months to gather my courage. I came without the kids, the suit, and the fanfare of Heidi's funeral. Today was about spending time alone, just Heidi and me.

As I sit here in my car next to her writing this post, I am overwhelmed with disbelief. I still cannot come to terms with the fact that she is here now only as an identifying nameplate on the ground.

I came here today and sat down on the small rocks above her grave. I didn't stay on the sidewalk; I had to somehow be closer to her. Sitting on the rocks helped. "If you touch a rock, it touches the ground, which touches her." I was overcome with emotions, crying uncontrollably. I guess this is to be expected.

I was glad I came without the kids for the first visit. I was able to say a few things to her. I assume she knows exactly how I feel, and she is watching how we are doing.

I looked down on her nameplate and couldn't help but focus on the years 1967 and 2015. The year she was born, and the year she died. This is so wrong.

I spoke to Chad this morning and let him know I was coming to visit his sister. He asked me to place a rock for him, so I did. Max knew I was coming this morning, and he asked me to bring Mom a Reese's peanut-butter cup from his Halloween bag. He knew that was her absolute favorite candy. So I brought that also. Finally, because I wanted to save our Disney rocks to lay as a family, I brought my own rock to mark that I was here and to give her my own hug. The two other rocks that were here let me know she has been visited by others. I am sure she takes great comfort in seeing everyone who comes by.

Heidi's connection to this world and to the life she had is now through dirt and rocks.

I am glad I came. It's reassuring knowing I can come here to reconnect with Heidi.

Heidi,

I miss you so much every single day. Life is hard without you. I am glad you finally have a peaceful place to rest, and I am glad that your dad is there with you to take care of you once again. I will see you again.

—Same.

November 7, 2015, 7:29 a.m. (Day 68)

Another week has passed. Another week of navigating this road by myself. I am on autopilot. I wake up, go to work, coordinate activities for the kids, RSVP for the kids to go to parties, figure out groceries, figure out what clothes the kids need and come up with a way to get them to a store, pay bills, get the dogs groomed, put gas in the car, have dinner, make school lunches, go to bed, and then start the routine all over again tomorrow. There is just not enough of me to go around.

In addition to all these things, there is still the task of keeping everyone's mental well-being in check. That means fitting family group therapy into the mix, tuning in moment by moment to see if the kids need to talk about anything relating to their emotional status and stopping everything if there is a need, and managing my own constantly changing emotional status. It is all completely overwhelming. Every day is a struggle and still clouded in a loneliness that cannot be lifted. I'm a robot running through a program.

They say that things get better in time and that time is a healer. I do believe this to be true, but how much time must pass? How much time must go by before I can begin to feel like the person I was? How many more days of loneliness must I endure? When does this get better?

I am tired, and this new life is wearing me down.

November 8, 2015, 5:25 p.m. (Day 69)

I feel conflicted. Today, Judy and I went to see a movie, just to get away and have some grownup time. On the way home I was driving, and Judy had to remind me to make the left turn toward our street. Heidi and I laughed about my navigational sense all the time. When I drove down the freeway she would remind me to take the next exit. Then, of course, I would give her "the look." She used to say that she was damned if she did and damned if she didn't. If she told me to exit or turn, she got "the look" and a comment or two about how I knew that. If she didn't alert me to the next turn, I would drive right past it. Judy's reminder made me smile.

Back at the house, there were three sympathy cards, a JDRF donation notification, and a note from my health insurance provider with new insurance cards without Heidi's name on them.

There are so many little stories that make up our lives. There are so many little things that mean nothing to most, but mean the world to us. I saw the movie *Steve Jobs*, which made me think about this man who changed the world but sacrificed everything to do it, a man who has now had several movies made about him to remind us of the legacy he left behind after his passing. There is no movie about Heidi, no portrayal of her life, but I believe she left behind a legacy to this world we live in, even if in the little things she did, and I believe it took her passing for us all to see it clearly.

Heidi was a tremendous human being, and we were all blessed to have known her.

November 10, 2015, 9:07 a.m. (Day 71)

Last night I had my third Heidi dream. This one was not pleasant. Heidi and I were at a moment in time after her diagnosis and close to her death. It was past the point I dreaded. It was in a space where Heidi knew she was going to die, and there was nothing she or I could do about it. It was a bit of a reenactment of our cancer journey. She couldn't leave the house, and I was right there with her. She would look through the windows at the world as it traveled by her. It was a very lonely dream, as people came in and out like a revolving door but could offer no comfort. I could see the sadness and the fear on her face.

I'm so grateful that what occurred in this dream never came to be, that she was never told there was nothing that could be done. I am so grateful she never hung around the house just waiting to die.

In my adult group at the peer counseling I take the boys to, I met a guy named Mark. We shared a common journey and became friends quickly. Mark has also lost his wife to cancer and is now raising his son on his own. Mark and his wife chose to be fully informed about her prognosis and what the outcome and timing were likely to be; they faced it, accepted it, and prepared for it. They embraced the knowledge of her mortality, because it offered them time to prepare. This awareness allowed them an opportunity to communicate important information, clean up loose ends, and write a love note from mother to son. They were organized and very matter-of-fact about her upcoming passing. They made choices that worked for them.

Heidi's and my journey was very different. As Heidi hadn't researched her survival odds, hers was a path of positivity and hope, but with me along. The path that Heidi chose for us was not always easy. In particular, my decision to be with her so that she was never alone put me in a precarious situation with my job. Her diagnosis greatly reduced my hours and capacity to work. My business partners were patient and understanding at first, but by the sixth month, their patience began to run thin. I remember sitting at a lunch with them when they suggested I get a nurse. I simply explained, "That's not what she wants. She wants me." I couldn't bring in someone else to take care of her. The outcome of this battle was still unclear, and if these were the last days, weeks, or months that I was going to spend with Heidi, how did I want to spend them? Did I want to look back at this period of my life and say, "I worked!" Of course, work is still here.

November 12, 2015, 8:06 a.m. (Day 73)

I knew a day like this would come. Today Madeline woke up with a fever of 101.4°F, which means no school for her and no work for me. This is another hurdle we will need to jump over. Kids are going to get sick; things are going to happen that Heidi would have just taken care of.

This morning, while battling her fever and feeling a little nauseated, Madeline said something to me that set me back a little. She explained how being sick created a connection to Mom. Madeline put herself in Heidi's shoes and was affected. She expressed to me her disbelief about how sick Heidi had been and how she handled it for as long as she did.

Every experience we have is forever changed because of Heidi's passing. This was just a normal day of fever and not feeling well, and yet there is nothing normal about it.

November 14, 2015, 9:14 a.m. (Day 75)

Three stories about yesterday.

The first: I finalized plans and put deposits down to go on a cruise with the kids, Judy, and Chad and his family during spring break.

After Heidi and I got married in 1999, we went on a Caribbean cruise on the Grand Princess for our honeymoon. It was amazing. It was seven wonderful days with just Heidi and every pampering you could imagine. The food was incredible, the service was great, and the ports were outstanding. On that trip, I bought Heidi a little diamond tennis bracelet, tax free. Heidi and I took a picture together on "formal night" that still stands atop my dresser today. We also discovered "cruise hunger." This happens immediately after you have finished a big meal; you pass a hot dog stand or snack bar and although you're stuffed and can't handle another bite, you take one anyway because you just can't say no.

We had such a great time that afterward for years we wanted to go back and cruise again. Then we had kids, and that became a little hard to do at their young ages. As they grew, we wanted more than anything to take them on a cruise, but whenever we looked into it, it was always too expensive. We never made it back to a ship.

My desire to go back to sea hasn't left. As I was showing Judy the deck plans for the upcoming cruise, I realized this trip is not mine, it's ours—this is the repeat cruise that Heidi and I were never able to take together. Welcome aboard, my love.

As if the cruise revelation wasn't emotional enough, yesterday I received a return call from our dentist. A week or so ago I got a call from the dentist's office reminding Heidi to book an appointment. They knew about Heidi's cancer and referenced it in the message. I realized I never let them know, so I called the dentist a few days ago, and yesterday he got back to me. It is so hard communicating with someone who is experiencing the shock of hearing about Heidi's death for the first time. It's hard because, like so many others, our dentist was in disbelief. He kept repeating how heavy his heart was to hear this news. His grief was so fresh and raw. Heidi had been his patient for twenty-five years.

Lastly, as if all these emotions were not enough, yesterday my business partner sent out an announcement about our holiday party, being held on Saturday, December 19, exactly one year from Heidi's first oncologist appointment, the day after her tumors were discovered. I remember sitting in a waiting room that day while Heidi was getting a CT scan and seeing a woman walk by with the characteristic bandana covering her bald head. I remember staring at her, unable to turn away, and not being able to get my head around the fact that Heidi might soon be that woman. The email announcement about the party took me back to that day with laser precision.

All these experiences in one day—all driving home the fact that they are here but Heidi is not.

Chapter 21

Till Death Do Us Part

November 18, 2015, 4:01 a.m. (Day 79)

It's now around 4:00 a.m., the house is dark and quiet, the kids are asleep, and I find myself staring at a nondescript, circular band of gold molded to my left ring finger. The exterior is smooth and rounded, and the inside hides an inscription, "April 25, 1999," a date of celebration, my wedding date. For over sixteen years I have looked down at my finger and seen this ring.

In 1999, while most Americans were preparing for the end of the world, the looming technological Armageddon known as Y2K, Heidi and I were planning to become husband and wife. While others were building bomb shelters, hoarding gold, and buying guns, we were tasting cakes, auditioning music groups, and organizing seating charts. For months, my Type-A bride spent countless hours meticulously planning every detail. She picked the music to walk down the aisle to, coordinated the flowers to match the linens, and timed the flow of the meal, from appetizer to cake. No detail was left to the imagination.

On April 25, 1999, Heidi and I stood before many people and uttered the words "for better or worse" and "till death do us part." This was a promise I made to her. This was a promise I kept.

At the ceremony we were handed a pair of gold rings to exchange as a sign of our love and devotion to each other. Hers would accompany the engagement ring she already wore, and mine would wrap solo around my finger to always remind me of the woman who completed the story of my life. As the ring slid onto my finger, the world around me faded, and I looked into Heidi's eyes and saw her soul connect with mine. I was overtaken with a sense of purpose and joy. There are few perfect moments in life; this was one of them.

The day after Heidi's passing I had to go to the cemetery and make the arrangements. During this conversation I was asked about what kind of plot I wanted for her. I was offered a companion plot, with room above Heidi for another to be laid to rest. They explained that the spot above her didn't necessarily need to be used, meaning if I met someone else and decided to not be put to rest with Heidi, that was okay. I couldn't believe this was even being brought up; I am a very loyal person, and when I make a vow it's real. Just having this discussion felt like I was cheating on Heidi. However, it brought up a valid point. I am forty-seven years old, still very young. Am I supposed to remain alone for the rest of my life? Would Heidi want that for me? Would I want that for her? Probably not. That was a very awkward conversation.

This has also been one of my most difficult internal conversations. Emotionally, I still feel married, but physically, I feel I am not. All the joys of being married are gone. The joy of having someone to share everything with is gone. The physical joy of being able to touch, hold, or hug someone is gone. The joy of knowing you are with the someone you were meant to be with is gone.

How do you go on feeling married when you can't feel married?

For sixteen years, I have not taken off my wedding ring for more than a few minutes. I am still wearing it right now. I've had many thoughts about my ring and what it signifies. It is a symbol of marriage, relationship, and commitment. What is it a symbol of now? It is a symbol of what was but is physically no longer.

Removing my ring from my finger is an awful experience to contemplate, but it is one I've been thinking about a lot. When is the right time to do so? When is it socially acceptable to remove my ring? What does that even mean? Here are, once again, a combination of questions to which I have no answers.

I was not made to be alone. It is not in my DNA. More than money and more than success, I always wanted a family. I had it. Although I still have my three wonderful kids, my life is not the same without that grown-up someone to share it with.

Madeline has asked me on several occasions if I will get married again. It's a weird conversation to have less than three months out from Heidi's death. The reality is, maybe, probably, hopefully. I hope that I may find another, but again, when is the right time for that?

When is the right time for anything? I don't know, but I feel that maybe the time has come for me to remove my ring from my finger. What happens after that is unclear. Maybe the time has come to remove the symbol of my old life and come to terms with my new one—very reluctantly, mind you. I cannot escape the reality of my life without her. Perhaps it's right to put some of this behind me and continue my journey forward, even though it's hard.

I kept Heidi's wedding ring. I think it's time to put my ring with hers in a jewelry box, where we can be together physically once again. Let the symbols of our marriage remain together, but release myself onto my next chapter.

The fingers of my right hand grab the ring reluctantly; they begin to slide it off, and I feel the resistance. I'm removing sixteen years of happiness, memories, and contentment. I'm removing a symbol of a life that was and can never be again. My left hand will show the world that my marriage, as I knew it, is over.

During our wedding, the rabbi said, "Let these rings be an eternal sign of devotion, a lasting symbol of Heidi and Gregg's commitment to each other." That has not changed; my soul will always be connected to hers; I will always love, honor, and cherish her.

From the top drawer of my armoire, I pull out a small red jewelry box. Heidi's two rings rest on the velvet inside; the engagement ring with the single diamond and the gold wedding band next to it. I place my ring beside them so that the two wedding rings touch each other slightly. I catch a glimpse of the date inscribed inside the two bands where they once rested against our fingers. I close the box, place it back into the drawer, and slide the drawer closed. Like an amputee, I can still feel the touch of gold, but I know there is nothing there.

November 20, 2015, 10:21 a.m. (Day 81)

It seems that my prior post about removing my ring has sparked some opinions, concerns, and comments.

"Most people continue to wear their ring until they find someone else they want in their life! Not sure I understand!"

"Do not do things until things feel comfortable; what is the rush?"

"My guess is that certain things will *never* feel comfortable. Gregg is going at the pace that he needs to. But that doesn't make it comfortable."

I'm sure there are more thoughts out there that have not been shared.

As I have moved through this process and chosen to do so publicly, I knew that there would come a time when I would open myself up to the court of public opinion. It appears that maybe that time has come.

Let me start off by saying one cannot erase eighteen years of feelings and sixteen years of marriage in three months. Removing my ring, a symbol of what was, in no way removes the emotions of my life with Heidi. It is a weird feeling to feel married but not have a spouse.

A wedding ring is a public symbol of a pairing; it's a sign of something that physically no longer exists for me. I don't need a ring to know the relationship I had with Heidi, to maintain that heartfelt connection with her. My ring belongs with hers.

Removing it was no easy decision. There are societal norms that will put others in a position of judgment, but have those who judge walked this path? Please find me the rule book on how to move forward, and I will follow the rules. There cannot be a right or wrong, there is only what shows up. I don't know if the time for this was "the right time." When is that? Tell me, and I will react accordingly.

Here is the truth: I loved and love Heidi more than anything, except for maybe my kids. The truth is, she is gone, and that changes my life exponentially. I have no idea what tomorrow looks like.

I will continue to journal this journey. I will continue to welcome all opinions, both positive and negative. I truly appreciate everyone's reactions, comments, and likes.

For now, I have put away my ring with Heidi's, and I will take comfort in that symbolism.

Chapter 22

The Fifth Wheel

November 22, 2015, 8:49 a.m. (Day 83)

I am starting to believe that the hardest part of this journey is dealing with the loneliness. Loneliness is always just below the surface, waiting to be released. I can keep it under control by working, running errands, and generally staying busy, but the moment I stop, it escapes and takes over.

Yesterday was the perfect example of this. Jack had to be at his football game at 7:30 a.m. and back home around 9:00. I Dropped the dogs off to be groomed at 10:30, then drove Jack and Madeline to tennis by 11:00. While they were at tennis, I shopped for groceries at two different stores and ordered Madeline's birthday cake for next weekend. I picked up Madeline and Jack at 12:30, grabbed lunch, went home and caught my breath for about twenty minutes. Then the phone rang; the dogs were ready. I picked up the dogs, brought them home, and turned around to get Max from a birthday party early so I could get him to his football game by 4:15 p.m. Watched his game, went home, sent Madeline off with a friend for the evening, and took the two boys out to dinner. That was my weekend/unwind-from-work day.

At dinner, things finally started to relax and calm down. Dinner was nothing out of the norm, except it was with a ten-year-old and a twelve-year-old. They were on their iPads in whatever game land they live in, and I was on the other side of the table with me, myself, and I. This is nothing new for us. The kids generally play on their devices until the food comes, then all devices are put down. It's just that in the past they would play and Heidi and I would chat. It can make for a long dinner when you are sitting alone. I know I can remove the devices from dinner; we do at home. The boys and I did engage, but it isn't the same.

November 26, 2015, 2:01 p.m. (Day 87)

Thanksgiving has arrived. It's a day I've been apprehensive about and dreading, with great potential to be a very tough day. So far, it hasn't been much of a day at all. It's not happy, and it's not sad. I am rather numb to the whole experience. Perhaps this is a good thing.

Yesterday was a tougher day than today. Today I will spend time with my parents—who came up from Tucson—and with Judy and the kids. Tonight, Madeline and I will go out and face the crowds for early shopping bargains. She will occupy the space her mother filled so many times in the past. I'm glad she's coming.

I remember last Thanksgiving, after dinner, Heidi and I went out and walked Target, Walmart, and Best Buy. By this time last year Heidi was already experiencing discomfort due to what she thought was a pulled muscle. I remember being happy that Heidi was out with me despite her discomfort. Walking the stores, just the two of us, was something we really enjoyed. It was always fun to come back with bags filled with great bargains. Last year's great find was a set of ten pairs of girls' socks for $5, which was just what we needed for Madeline's bat mitzvah. We got twelve sets.

We always spent Black Friday together as a family. We went from store to store, with the kids in tow. I know Heidi and I liked this day much more than the kids did; however, we all went together. Tomorrow Madeline and I will pair up to tackle the mall and see what deals we can get. The boys will go fishing with their grandpa at a local lake. My family has divided, and I guess I'm okay with it.

So today is Thanksgiving. What is there to be thankful for? Even in this cloud I walk through daily there is always something to be thankful for. I know it is cliché to say, but I am truly thankful for my kids and for the great people they are becoming. I am thankful for eighteen years with Heidi. I am thankful that she is no longer suffering.

Today is another day of going through the motions, another day I will face and get through wondering what tomorrow looks like. Today is one of many firsts and one of many milestones. Yet today is just another day.

November 29, 2015, 7:19 a.m. (Day 90)

It's early morning, and there are eight teenage girls asleep on my family room floor. Last night was Madeline's birthday celebration. Today is Madeline's fourteenth birthday. One of the things she told me is that she really wanted to wake up on her birthday with her friends here to greet her. She will get that.

Yesterday Madeline was very busy. She was cleaning the house, blowing up balloons, and hanging streamers. These were the things that Heidi always did for the kids on their birthdays. Heidi always made such a big deal out of everyone's birthday. She said everyone is entitled to at least one very special day.

By the time Madeline's friends arrived yesterday, our house rivaled even the best party room at Chuck E. Cheese. She was focused and excited. Her excitement increased when everyone arrived, and it continued throughout the night, across the grounds of Castles & Coasters, and then back at the house. It was almost 2:00 a.m. when they all finally ran out of steam and fell asleep. Madeline had a great night.

Last night, as Judy and I were sitting and waiting for the guests to arrive, I was amazed with how well Madeline was handling this first birthday without her mother. I found myself looking on, waiting for some emotion to hit Madeline and bring her down. It never came. Perhaps it will arrive after her friends leave, perhaps not. Grieving is such an individual journey.

My kids continue to amaze me. They have been so resilient. On the surface, they have managed this journey seemingly better than I have.

Perhaps there is a gift of youth that allows them to do so. I don't know, but I'm glad that whatever is driving them has allowed them to continue being kids. I'm glad they are finding strength, wherever it is coming from. I'm proud of all three of them. Their strength gives me strength. When I know they're okay, I know I'm okay.

I think birthdays will always have just a little more meaning now. They are important. Birthdays need to be welcomed and celebrated, because you never know when birthdays may run out.

Chapter 23

Happy Birthday

December 1, 2015, 9:23 p.m. (Day 92)

I know I keep saying that today was a tough day, but today was a very tough day. It wasn't a day filled with depression that overwhelmed me, or a day where every minute I wallowed in misery. It was just a tough day. Today was my forty-eighth birthday.

So many people wrote on my wall and wished me a happy birthday. I don't think I've ever had so many people take time out to recognize me on my birthday. Thank you to everyone. It is your support that continues to lift me up when I am down.

Today was shadowed by so many thoughts and visions. Heidi's birthday is August 1, exactly four months earlier than mine. We were born in the same year, but for as long as I can remember I would tease her about being my old lady. I would always tell her that her birthday started the best four months of the year. I would tease her that when she was in her fifties I would still be in my forties. Of course that joke didn't quite play out. There has been nothing fun or humorous about these last four months. They have been the worst of my life.

December 5, 2015, 4:11 a.m. (Day 96)

I miss Heidi.

I miss talking to her about anything and everything.

I miss having her complete my sentence.

I miss her sense of humor.

I miss that she got my sense of humor.

I miss running errands together.

I miss wanting to go see a movie with her (and it could only be a comedy or a romantic comedy).

I miss not knowing where to go for lunch but finding a place to have lunch with her, nonetheless.

I miss having someone on the other side of my bed (sorry Max).

I miss just being the driver.

I miss calling her from work or being called.

I miss her voice on the voicemail.

I miss being edited and corrected.

I miss that she knew everything technical and was frustrated that I didn't.

I miss her organizational skills.

I miss sitting next to her.

I miss getting emails that are signed "same."

I miss being asked to watch an "us" show, when almost all the shows she liked to watch were anything but "us."

I miss her complaining about having to pluck her face.

I miss being bored waiting for her in a clothing store while she tried on half the store only to go home with one, maybe two things.

I miss the comfort and security our relationship provided.

I miss laughing.

I miss having a mother for my kids.

I miss her not turning off the lights in the house after she left a room.

I miss getting through a day or a week without crying because there was no reason to do so.

I miss her Type-A+ personality.

I miss being able to say "I love you" to her every night before going to sleep.

I miss not feeling alone.

I miss leaving the kids at home and having a date night.

I miss being able to kiss and hug my wife.

I miss companionship.

I miss having grown-up conversations about kids, work, and life.

I miss waking up in the morning and taking for granted everything I had.

I miss the boring, routine life we had.

I miss hearing how the house was always dirtier than it was.

I miss grocery shopping and only pushing the cart.

I miss going on trips as a family of five.

I miss not squeezing into a four-top table at restaurants.

I miss seeing how happy she was to just be a mom and a wife.

I miss her taking a week to pack for us to go away for a week.

I miss cooking well-done steaks.

I miss everything about the life I had.

I miss Heidi!

Chapter 24

Circles

December 10, 2015, 9:38 a.m. (Day 101)

My life seems to be a series of circles.

This morning, after dropping off Max at school, I went to CVS pharmacy because I needed to get a portable needle clipper for Jack. A seemingly simple task. As I pulled up to the store, I was hit by memories of the last time I was there, August 29, and the kindness of the pharmacist.

Heidi needed some medical equipment to make her more comfortable. By this time she was so weak she was having trouble getting herself up in the bathroom, so I was looking for an elevated toilet seat with handles. She also wasn't getting out of bed much, so I bought a foam bed wedge to help her sit up.

Lastly, she was experiencing a lot of pain, so I bought a large ice pack she could put on her lower back, which seemed to help. I remember the woman who helped me pick out these items so clearly. As I know I've mentioned, she helped me to my car with the new in-home care goods and asked if she could give me a hug, which she did. Two days later, Heidi passed away.

What that woman did was a random act of kindness that still means so much to me today, almost four months later. She wasn't there this morning, and I can't remember her name. She made an impact on me, and I feel I need to find her and tell her.

The past two weeks have been very hard to get through: I have had Thanksgiving, Madeline's birthday, my birthday, and now Hanukkah. Any one of these would be hard enough to go through without Heidi here. Having all of them within such a short period of time has been like being in a boxing match with no guard up. I keep getting hit.

I haven't been sleeping well, and I'm tired all the time. I can't seem to focus in or out of work. I am once again wearing my "everything is all right" mask, but it isn't. I am tired of putting every ounce of strength I have into just getting through the days, and I am tired of grieving.

I am ready for something different.

December 15, 2015, 10:41 p.m. (Day 106)

Yesterday I was on my phone deleting text messages I no longer needed, and I stumbled across one that I sent to Trina, the nurse who took such good care of Heidi those days in the hospital just before her passing. In this text was a photo of Heidi and Trina on the hospital bed posing for the camera. This photo was taken the Friday before her passing and it's the last one I have of her alive. My eyes were fixed to this photo for what must have been ten or fifteen minutes. I couldn't stop looking at it. Heidi wore her typical smile to show the world everything was all right. I stared at this photo in disbelief that at that moment in time, we had fewer than three days left together.

It's so strange to look at a snapshot of a moment in time and remember just how innocent life can be. Time and memory are such crazy mind tricks.

Today, I went to my primary care doctor for the first time in almost six years (yeah, I know!). I went because I have to focus on my own health so I can focus on the health of my family. I have to start taking care of me because I need to take care of my kids. There is no one else.

Heidi and I had the same primary care doctor. As I walked into the doctor's office and sat down in the lobby waiting to be called, I was thinking of Heidi's visit there nearly a year ago for what she believed to be a pulled muscle. I felt her presence.

My physical went well, other than finding out that I'm beginning to shrink and need to lose more than a few pounds. Everything else is fine.

December 18, 2015, 11:41 p.m. (Day 109)

Exactly one year ago today was the day Heidi was told her liver had tumors. I remember it as if it were yesterday. That was the beginning of the end. Tomorrow would be her first oncologist appointment, Tuesday her biopsy day, next Wednesday her diagnosis day, Thursday her first chemo treatment in the hospital, and so on and so on. All these anniversaries lead up to August 31, 2016, the worst anniversary of them all.

December 23, 2015, 5:23 p.m. (Day 114)

I thought I was doing pretty well. It appeared that the anticipation of these anniversaries I am currently in the middle of was worse than I actually felt, and that I was managing these dates quite well, all things considered. Then lunch happened.

Today was my office lunch/holiday party. It was held at the same restaurant as last year. I was talking with one of my colleagues, who was comparing this year to last year, and it hit me. Last year, while my office was enjoying a nice lunch, I was at the oncologist's with Judy and Heidi. I almost had to excuse myself so I didn't start to cry. It took every ounce of energy I had to keep wearing my "everything is all right" mask. Every day still requires so much effort.

December 24, 2015, 8:09 a.m. (Day 115)

Christmas Eve 2014 was the day Heidi checked into the hospital to begin her chemo treatments. We had just received the cancer diagnosis the night before, so there was absolutely no time to come to terms with what a cancer diagnosis even meant. There was no time to get our heads around it. Diagnosed last night, in the hospital today.

I documented the journey with photos. The fear and anxiety on Heidi's face was evident. One of the first things they had to do was give Heidi a port. What the hell is a port? We were told that the port was how she would receive her chemo. We were also told that it needed to be surgically implanted under her skin in her upper chest area, and it would remain there until all her treatments were completed. Even though Heidi had had three C-sections, surgery was one of her greatest concerns and fears. So right away she was faced with fear number one.

Once the port was in, her chemo treatments could begin. She was scheduled for six. Each treatment cycle would be the same: three days long. The first session would last approximately eight hours, the next for two hours, and the third two hours as well. Then the process would repeat three weeks later.

We get information about chemo from TV, movies, and what you hear from someone who knew someone who went through it, but you still have no idea what the treatment will be. You hear how tough it is and how sick it makes people, but hearing about it and facing it are two different things.

I can't imagine how Heidi found the courage to face a treatment well known for being brutal and with all kinds of side effects. I remember watching Heidi with a chemo bag hooked up to her, internally shaking my head in disbelief. How did we get here? Where did this come from? Why her? The days were long, the nights were long, and every hour was filled with concern and worry.

These are the thoughts running through my head this Christmas Eve, one year later. These memories will scar me for as long as I live. Christmas was always a day to go see a movie and eat Chinese food, not for beginning chemo.

December 24, 2015, 3:58 p.m. (Day 115)

For the last couple of hours, Judy and I have been going through file cabinets in my garage. As I removed the files Heidi kept on the kids and began to go through them, I was reminded of what an amazing mother she was. There was art from preschool and pictures of her with Madeline and Jack when they were Star of the Week. She tried to never miss an event. She kept everything. Her children were the world to her. There was nothing more important than being there for them. She created an environment filled with love and happiness. As I write this, I can hear the kids laughing in the other room as they read the notes they wrote when they were three and four years old. These moments are priceless, and it's so sad that Heidi isn't here to share in this happiness she created by saving these precious gems, or to see what kind of human beings they are to become.

I cannot replace Heidi. I cannot replace their mother.

December 29, 2015, 9:22 a.m. (Day 120)

Never go to bed angry. I know this is age-old advice, and I know that if we could live by this rule, we would all be better people. Last night was a real struggle to live by this rule.

Although I didn't go to bed angry, I did go to bed very disturbed. This has been a tough winter break to negotiate emotionally, the first without Heidi. What does that mean besides the obvious? It means that while I am working, there is no other parent to be with my kids. For two-and-a-half weeks my kids have to spend more time than they're used to on their own. My kids are independent and trustworthy. They are great kids, but Heidi's not being around for them has affected me.

In the past, if they wanted to have friends over or go somewhere during break, Heidi was available to handle that. Heidi could host, make lunch, or take them somewhere. Not this year. They have had to fend for themselves, and it's created a lot of pressure on me to better manage my work and my parenting obligations.

Last night it all came to a climax. For days now, Madeline has been asking to have a few friends over for yet another sleepover. The best denial I could come up with was "because," though the real reason was that it is just too hard to manage my every day, my work, the kids, the groceries, the shopping, and everything else that needs to happen to keep this family going. By the end of the day I just want some quiet time to recover.

As much as I like her friends and my boys' friends, I just don't want them overnight. When I told Madeline last night, she kept pushing and pushing for a better reason. I got frustrated, and it took everything I had not to blow up at her. She said to me over and over, "Is it because of Mom?"

In many ways, it is because of Heidi being gone, and I just didn't want to put myself in a position where I may have admitted that aloud. It was a hard night, and I feel bad about it. It's not easy to be a fourteen-year-old girl, and it's not easy to be a fourteen-year-old girl's single dad.

December 31, 2015, 8:10 p.m. (Day 121)

"Happy New Year!"—I've heard this all day. It's a wish so many in the world are excited to relay to one another. Tonight is a night of creating and committing to resolutions, and watching an electronic ball drop over Times Square in New York.

Happy New Year is something I wish I were feeling. I'll admit I am glad to get out of 2015, which turned out to be the worst year of my life: It gave me grief on such an enormous scale, it is almost unrecoverable; it tested me in ways I never thought possible, taking me to the edge of darkness and pushing me right through it. This year has shown me just how many tears the human body is capable of producing, and then it produced more. Tonight, I'll try and stay up until just before midnight, and then I will walk outside and give 2015 a huge middle finger salute.

The only New Year's resolution I have is to get through one day at a time.

So I say, "Happy New Year," and I will try to believe it.

January 1, 2016, 12:25 a.m. (Day 122)

The ball just dropped, and it is officially 2016. As soon as the clock struck twelve, I started to cry. It was as if the tension of an entire year released at once. The boys stayed up to see the ball drop, and after it did, Jack also expressed how bad 2015 was and that he is glad to be out of it.

Here is to a new year and a new beginning. May it bring peace and healing to me and my family. We sure can use some.

January 3, 2016, 11:18 a.m. (Day 124)

What does it mean to love someone? I think love can be measured by the feelings that show up after a loss. I loved Heidi with all my heart and with everything I have. I know this because it hurts so much now that she's gone. Sometimes, I find myself completely overtaken with grief, sadness, and pain. Sometimes, this happens for no apparent reason, like this morning. I just did the simple task of going grocery shopping, and on my way back I started crying. The tears ran down my cheeks, not because I heard a song or remembered something, not because someone said something to me or I saw somebody who triggered a memory. I started to cry because it was Sunday at 11:00 in the morning. I started to cry just because.

January 9, 2016, 11:14 p.m. (Day 130)

Today was one of those days when nothing went right. I was going to take the kids to an outlet mall with some friends, but our friends were unable to go at the last minute. That wasn't a big deal; I decided to just take the kids by myself and make a day of it. Well, that plan quickly turned south.

We were late getting out of the house and on a tight schedule because Max had to be back for an afternoon football game. So right away, the day started off stressfully. Because of the late start, we had to pick a fast food restaurant for lunch, not a nicer sit-down place. Of course, the restaurant I chose was not on the kids' list, so the little one decided he wasn't going to eat anything. After a few minutes of a tantrum he finally came around—until his kid's cup came without a straw; then the world collapsed again. By this time, I was beginning to feel my blood boil and debated not going shopping at all, but there wasn't another good day this whole month to knock out this trip, so we continued.

On the car ride down, Madeline and I had a little power struggle about whose music we should listen to; of course, I won. Upon arrival, Madeline wanted to go into girl stores, and the boys wanted to go into boy stores, so that stirred up a nice sibling battle. This trip was one argument after another.

Madeline argued with Jack, Jack argued with Max, Max argued with Madeline. I can handle it when one of the kids is a little out of control, but when all three are out of control it makes me want new kids. Finally, two-and-a-half hours later, the bickering was over, and we headed home. Shortly into the drive, the battle of the music began. I won again. After a long, silent car ride we finally arrived at home just in time to drop the two older ones off and get to Max's football game. The game was nice; they won, and Max had a great time. After the game, he wanted to go to his friend's house for a sleepover. Why does everything have to be a sleepover? I am plagued by sleepovers!

Once again, the timing was not going to work out, so I denied the sleepover. Well, here came evil Max. More mad looks, more disobedience, and more of me being the worst dad ever. By the time I got home I was spent. I had to run away. Madeline made plans to go ice skating with friends, and those plans coordinated perfectly with a movie. Yay! So I took Madeline to her evening event, and as soon as we got in the car she demanded money. She didn't ask, she told me to give her some. Crappy day still going, just like the Energizer bunny. I gave her $20 and dropped her off; she slammed my car door shut when she exited. Finally, some peace.

Off to the movies I went, by myself. The movie was packed; by the time I got there it was over 80 percent sold. I know this because I asked. No problem when you only need one seat. I found a "buffer" seat between two couples. I sat and prepared to enjoy my time away from my tyrannical children.

The younger couple to my right was very touchy-feely and cuddly. They held hands, they sat close, and she leaned back into him for most of the movie. Nothing bad and nothing annoying, but I can never escape my own situation. Heidi and I had been that touchy-feely, cuddly couple. When we saw movies, we usually put up the armrest between us.

I'd have my hand on her leg or hers on mine. We'd hold hands, and for much of the movie she would lean back into me. It was really nice to have that closeness. It made movie-watching great, even if the movie was a chick flick or romantic comedy.

I found myself fixated on the couple as much as the movie. It was hard to see a couple so happy together.

No matter what I do or where I go, I'm constantly reminded of what I have lost. Simple things are not so simple. A movie is not just a movie.

January 12, 2016, 2:33 a.m. (Day 133)

Every morning my alarm goes off at 3:00 a.m. so I can test Jack's blood sugar numbers. I do this because Type 1 diabetes is unpredictable and dangerous and anything can happen overnight. I've done this for years. Why am I writing about this at 2:20 in the morning? Tonight at 2:14 a.m. I felt the tapping of a finger on my left shoulder. I sleep on my right side. It tapped me three times. *Tap tap tap.* At first I thought it was Max, again in my bed and waking me for some reason. I turned over, but no one was there. Puzzled, I looked over at the clock and decided, rather than wait until 3:00, I would go check Jack right then since I was sort of up anyway. I was stunned to discover his blood sugar was at 31, which is very dangerously low—seizures can happen around 30! I am sure that tapping on my shoulder was Heidi. Heidi, the ultimate Type-1 mom, was looking out for her son.

Thanks for the assist.
—Same.

Chapter 25

The Grief Wubby

January 18, 2016, 7:43 p.m. (Day 139)

How do you sum up someone in two lines? How do you describe forty-eight years of a person in two lines? This is what I was asked to do today. Today, I had to finish the second part of a burial; I had to go back to the cemetery and finalize arrangements for Heidi's headstone.

Tuesday after Heidi passed away, when I was in the cemetery office last, we briefly touched on the topic of the headstone. It took mere seconds for me to choose the stone. The right one was obvious. Then I was asked what I would like to say on the headstone. I had two lines I could fill to describe Heidi. Two lines. I couldn't do it. The epitaph would have to wait.

Today was just a matter of signing the paperwork and paying; I still couldn't face writing an epitaph. Judy and both boys accompanied me. As soon as I entered the office, I was immediately reminded of the rawness of that day some five months ago.

This was also the first time the boys had come to see their mother. We proceeded to Heidi's grave and gave Heidi her rocks from Disneyland. Madeline chose not to come; I guess she's not ready. I understand. Visiting Heidi's grave is such a hard thing to do. It puts me face to face with how much I miss her.

January 24, 2016, 3:17 p.m. (Day 145)

Today is a big football day. The Cardinals play the Panthers to see who goes to the Super Bowl. Max had a doubleheader of two flag football games. Max's team dominated. They won the first game 33–6. They won the second game 44–0. On the way home from the second game, Max was on cloud nine. He was so excited. He told me how he put on a show for me today. Then he said he put on a show for Mom also, and that he puts on a show for Mom every game.

I always wonder how the kids are doing, because they're so collected on the surface. It's comments like these that remind me Heidi's death affects us all on so many levels. It's not just me who must figure out ways to get through every day, it's the kids as well. It's Heidi's "momma's boy," Max, who has to find ways to stay in touch with his mom any way he can. I'm sure Heidi is looking down and enjoying the shows Max puts on for her every week.

January 29, 2016, 3:50 a.m. (Day 150)

My posts seem to be stretching further apart; more time seems to be passing in between. Since my posts are directly related to the emotions of my loss that continue to show up, I suppose I should view this as a mild sign of some sense of healing.

It's been five months since Heidi's passing, and although I still miss her every day, I can feel the waves of grief getting farther apart. Of course, all could change later today or tomorrow. I accept this move forward as a mixed bag. The waves of grief that overtake me are difficult to endure. They overwhelm me and leave me exhausted. Yet, in a strange way, these waves keep me connected to Heidi. They remind me of the life I had and keep me close to it.

As much as I want, and need, to move beyond my past, I never want to lose touch with the relationship Heidi and I had. I know I will never forget, but as time moves on, the bond we shared becomes more of a memory and less concrete. It's getting harder to remember her face or the sound of her voice. It's hard to live through. I want to hold on to my grief like a soft blanket, but I know at some point I have to let my blanket go and put it behind me. At some point, I will have to open myself up to meeting someone else. As one foot enters the future, my other foot is still planted in the past. I am doing splits, and I hope I don't fall down.

Later today I will fly to Las Vegas to enjoy a weekend reunion with thirteen of my fraternity brothers from college. My fraternity brother "Stain," seeing how awful I looked at the shiva, suggested a weekend in Vegas. What was going to be a trip with a few has turned into a reunion of many. I haven't seen many of these guys in over twenty years.

Heidi has brought my old friendships back to the forefront of my life. Still, the voice in my head says, "How dare you feel good so close to Heidi's death!" My logical brain wags its finger at me and criticizes my feelings. I am in tremendous conflict. It's hard to see my life with Heidi only through the rear-view mirror. It's hard to keep driving alone.

Chapter 26

Swiping Right

February 8, 2016, 4:29 a.m. (Day 160)

As this process of posting and journaling has progressed, I've asked myself if there is any personal experience I'm having that would be publicly off limits. My answer has continuously been no. Toward the beginning of this journey I decided I would share my experiences as they happened in whatever raw form they took. As a result of this openness, I feel I have received therapeutic benefits that have saved me thousands of dollars in therapy hours. Today's post has become a tough one for me to open up and write about, but here it is.

For a little while now I have been hiding in the shadows on a dating site. I haven't been public about it, and I haven't revealed myself on the site. Several days ago as I was viewing a profile that caught my attention, I accidentally sent a flirt. This is a symbol to show interest and invite a conversation. It happened because I am completely technically impaired, and I was exploring some of the features and scrolled over the flirt to see what it was. What I didn't know is that when you do that it automatically releases and sends the flirt. I guess curiosity kills the cat every time. Well, because I did it, my cover was blown. There was no way to take the flirt back. I was officially out of the shadows.

A day later my flirt received a response. This experience was like sending a signal into outer space and getting a response from an alien life force. So as not to be rude, I responded and began a conversation. I was as nervous as a high schooler. I haven't spoken to another woman under dating circumstances in over eighteen years. All kinds of questions were going through my mind. Am I ready to go down this road? What do I tell the kids? What do I tell Judy? It's only been five months; am I allowed to begin a search for another? The dating scene is hard enough without all these extra parameters. I think, just maybe, this is another part of the healing process and moving forward. Maybe this is a first step to moving toward a space where grief and happiness can coexist with each other. Maybe it is okay to work toward being happy again?

February 11, 2016, 9:20 a.m. (Day 163)

I can sense myself changing. I feel that perhaps I am starting to emerge from this long dark tunnel. Maybe I'm beginning to come to terms with Heidi's passing. I think about her every day. I miss her every day.

I haven't had a gut-wrenching, can't-stop-crying moment in several weeks now. For this I'm thankful, as I know it's a sign of healing. In a strange way, I am missing being an emotional wreck. When I was an emotional wreck, her presence was with me; now it's more distant. I know this is probably normal and good, but I miss those overwhelming feelings.

For months, I've been saying I cannot predict what tomorrow will bring. I may be good today, but tomorrow I may be a mess. I've been living in the moment because moments change. It feels like, maybe, tomorrow might be turning into just another day.

Disclaimer: I reserve the right to be completely incorrect about all this and to have a complete emotional breakdown at any given moment.

February 12, 2016, 8:47 p.m. (Day 164)

Perhaps I spoke too soon. Tonight, Judy, the kids, and I went to Friday night services to celebrate the beginning of the bar mitzvah weekend for one of our closest friends. It's been a long time since I've been to services. It was nice to see Jack's best friend up in front of the congregation doing his thing. The service wasn't out of the ordinary, there was no special discussion or sermon, and the songs and Hebrew prayers were the same as they've always been. So what made tonight different? I spent the entire service fighting back tears, thinking of Heidi and our family.

There was something about tonight I can't put my finger on, but it was very emotional for me. The service included the "Mourner's Kaddish," the Jewish prayer for the loved ones we have lost, just like it always does. This prayer tonight took me right back to my living room every night for six nights in early September during the shiva for Heidi. Throughout the service I kept thinking to myself, "How am I going to get through Jack's bar mitzvah if I can barely get through this one?"

This is that grief thing coming right back into my face and slapping me for getting too comfortable without it.

February 17, 2016, 4:44 p.m. (Day 169)

I am beside myself once again. I'm sitting at my desk in my office, fighting back tears (and losing the fight). One of the tasks I had yet to complete was to come up with the "Endearment" for Heidi's headstone. That is the term used for the words that will be placed on the stone to give all who visit her a summation of her life. My challenge was to sum up an entire person in two lines or less. I've been struggling to find the right words. I even went and got a book from my rabbi to find inspiration. Nothing was coming to me.

Then, just a few minutes ago, the words arrived, at my desk, in the middle of my work day. It was gut-wrenching. This emotional outburst let me know I had the right words for her and reminded me how incomplete my life is right now. I wrote:

"She was a mother, a wife, a daughter, a sister and a friend. She did for others more than she would do for herself. She was a woman of valor."

Rest in peace, my beloved Heidi.

Chapter 27

Build Experiences, Build Memories

February 24, 2016, 9:29 a.m. (Day 176)

For the last several days, I have reverted into memories of Heidi—images of her coming to the surface. I've been reminded of what it was like to have Heidi around. At the grocery store. Riding in the passenger seat. Sitting across from me at the dinner table.

My snapshot memories of her seem far too real. I'm in disbelief that she has been taken away from us and that my kids don't have a mother; that of all the cancer survival stories you hear, we don't have one. I am in disbelief that I am stepping forward alone.

March 4, 2016, 7:36 a.m. (Day 185)

The clothes-shopping is over. The list-making and packing is over. Today we leave for Florida to board a ship and go on the biggest family vacation we've ever done. Now that all the pre-planning and preparations are finished, I've had a chance to reflect. My thoughts have been filled with irony. This would be the cruise Heidi and I wanted for ourselves and then for our children, but never had the means to do. We will leave to go on that mega-ship we always dreamed of. The irony is that without Heidi's passing and the existence of a life insurance policy, this dream trip would still be out of reach.

I have mentioned many times before how challenging it has become to accept good things I experience. It's challenging to fully enjoy positive experiences that are solely possible because of the horrific negative of Heidi's passing. This trip is one of those positive/negative relationships, and I am feeling it today.

One of Heidi's mantras was always "Build experiences, build memories." One can have the big house, one can have the fancy car, one can have a lot of expensive jewelry. All these things can be taken away or lost. What can never be taken away are experiences and memories sharing great times with family. This is what we will be doing today. We will create new family experiences and memories. We will do it in honor and memory of Heidi, who is in our hearts.

March 10, 2016, 7:00 a.m. (Day 191)

Through the wonders of very expensive, pay-per-day onboard Wi-Fi, I am able to log in and write this post. Right now, I am in the middle of the Atlantic Ocean on the first of two full days at sea heading back to Fort Lauderdale. The cruise has been everything I had hoped it would be, and more; it has become a turning point in my grief journey.

The kids are having an incredible time; this ship is amazing. The highlight so far has been our trip to Atlantis on Nassau, our first day. The water park there was so much fun! Except for my little mishap where I almost broke my foot and took a large portion of skin off my ankle on the "lazy" river, that was our best day. The ship has a great medical facility on board, which I have now visited three times to get fresh dressings over my ankle.

After leaving Ft. Lauderdale, our ship docked in Nassau around 8:00 a.m. It was scheduled to depart at 1:30 that afternoon. For years, I had seen TV commercials advertising the Atlantis Paradise Island resort and casino in the Bahamas. It showcased beautiful beaches and a world-renowned water park with water slides so steep, it appeared you were jumping and falling, not sliding.

And now, there we were, departing the ship and boarding a shuttle bus to Atlantis Paradise Island. The timing and cost of admission had given me pause. Much to my disappointment, the water park didn't open until 10:00 a.m., and entry fees were $450 for the four of us. For us to be back at the ship on time, we would have to leave no later than 12:30. Four-hundred fifty dollars for two and a half hours seemed hard to justify. But then I heard Heidi's voice in my head, "Build experiences and build memories." I forged ahead, knowing she'd want us to have the experience of a lifetime.

The water park was incredible. Our first stop was the Leap of Faith waterslide. World-famous, it boasts a sixty-foot, near-vertical drop. The four of us approached this behemoth gazing upward; it towered above the water park like a skyscraper. As we got closer, our group splintered; Madeline was several steps behind the rest of us, eyes focused on the tower before us, protesting loudly, "I'm not doing that—no way!" After several minutes of trying to convince her otherwise, the boys and I left her by the exit pool and continued onward. Jack was the first to take the plunge, then Max and then me. As Jack threw himself down the slide, Max and I could hear his screams, which grew fainter as Jack slid farther down. We hoped they were screams of excitement, but at the time it was unclear. After watching big brother, Max began to lose his courage and looked at me plaintively, as if hoping I might save him, but it was too late. He was next in line, and we were committed. As he plummeted, once again, I followed his screaming down the slide. Now it was my turn to hurl myself down this seven-story structure. As I slid, I felt myself freefall on a cushion of water and then level off into a clear, acrylic tunnel running through a shark-filled lagoon. So much water was being kicked up into my face, I couldn't see the sharks through the tube; that part had looked much better on TV. Upon my exit, Jack and Max were giddy with excitement, verbally reenacting the last few minutes of their lives. Seeing that all three of us had survived was enough to sway Madeline into trying it. As a group, the four of us went back to do it again, Madeline holding my hand and arm in a death grip the entire way up.

We continued through the park as rapidly as we could, in order to experience as many slides as possible in the two and a half hours we had.

After conquering the Leap of Faith, there was no holding us back. One slide raced two of us head-to-head, and another plunged us down fifty feet, spiraling through complete darkness. Another slide moved us directly from one ride into another. Upon completion of that slide, we found ourselves in Atlantis's version of what I mistakenly thought to be a "lazy river," but this river was anything but lazy. In fact, as it turns out, this ride was really called the Current, and for good reason. It started off calm and tranquil as we floated along in our inner tubes, but soon it became a mile-long journey through rolling waves and wild rapids.

For me, the river proved quite hazardous. At the beginning, I lost my balance and flipped over backward out of my tube. I went shooting through the shallow water and hit my head, hard, on the concrete surface below. I checked my head for bleeding and was relieved when I found none. I laughed it off and continued my journey. A short time later, I discovered I had a small, dime-size piece of skin missing from my knee; I laughed again. Farther along, I found myself in a more serious situation. My inner tube became caught in the current, turning in a circular motion, while my foot got stuck against the side, turning in the opposite direction. I was about to have a big problem. I grabbed my leg and forced my foot away from the wall, removing about an inch and a half of skin, several layers deep, over my ankle in the process. Once the fear and adrenaline subsided and I realized I hadn't broken my foot, I laughed at myself again. Now the kids were laughing at me as well. My ankle swelled and bruised, and for the next three days, I had to visit the medical facility on the ship to keep it wrapped and cleaned, but in that moment, I didn't care. I created a memory that the kids and I will enjoy with amusement for the rest of our lives.

And should our memories one day fail us, Atlantis made sure our day was immortalized in full color. Stationed around key areas of the park and throughout the river were employees with cameras ready to take pictures of your party and overcharge you to keep them. Of course, I bought them. I now have photos of each child, including Madeline, conquering their fears as they slid down the Leap of Faith. I have pictures of children stuffed into inner tubes like hermit crabs, giving me a thumbs-up just before being thrust into a tsunami. I have concrete reminders of a wonderful day, in a beautiful place with my kids, all because Heidi gave us the means to keep her mantra alive.

Two days after Nassau, we docked in St. Thomas for our scheduled beach day. St. Thomas is famous for Magens Bay, one of the most beautiful beaches in the Caribbean. Unfortunately, that day it was cloudy, windy, cold, and raining. Still, my attitude was, "Who cares?" While sitting at a small café on one of the main shopping streets, sipping frozen tropical drinks, I said to the kids; "The worst day in St. Thomas is better than the best day in Scottsdale. Why? Because we're in St. Thomas!" Damn the weather, we were going to the beach! The general had given the speech, and the troops were excited and ready for battle.

When we arrived, we established our claim with lawn chairs and towels; it wasn't exactly crowded. The water was still warm from the sunny day the island had enjoyed the day before. Raindrops bounced off the surface, and the boys wrestled with small but powerful waves. After a while, I went back up to the beach and took videos of my children playing in the ocean on a stormy day. The clouds didn't matter, the wind didn't matter, and the rain didn't matter. I was alone with my children, and we were having a fantastic time.

Yesterday, on one of our excursions into St. Maarten, I got into a conversation with two others on our little sailboat. It turns out that both of these ladies were diabetics, and they noticed Jack's pod, which started a conversation. We talked about all the challenges that one faces with this disease, different treatments, carb counts, and all the preparation it takes to travel. Throughout this conversation I found myself referencing all that Heidi had done to get us set up to manage this disease. I talked about her advocacy, her mentorship for newly diagnosed families, and more. The entire conversation was about Heidi in the present tense, as if she were right here beside me. Then it got weird. She isn't beside me, and she is not my ex-wife, so how could I speak so currently about someone who wasn't there? I started thinking about what they might have been thinking, and then out of nowhere I announced that Heidi passed away back in August. As soon as I did this, the entire tone of the conversation changed. It went to that awkward place where complete strangers don't know what to say, so they say the canned response, "Oh, I am so sorry to hear that." I know that people mean well, but it is still an emotionally awkward and heavy reaction to deal with. That is just my unwanted reality.

I think this cruise has helped me to evolve a little bit as well. The cruise is great, but everywhere you go you see complete families and couples. It is truly a direct, in-your-face, can't-hide-it visual. Everywhere I go, I am reminded of what I miss so much.

I am faced with finding ways to enjoy days and special events without that someone. I must find ways to enjoy moments by myself and with my kids and make those moments just as special and meaningful. This trip has helped me move a step closer to achieving that evolution, even though I know I still have many steps to go until I am truly there. One step forward.

March 11, 2016, 8:52 p.m. (Day 192)

Our cruise is coming to an end. Tomorrow morning we arrive back in Ft Lauderdale. Tonight we gathered as a family and honored Heidi. It was special. Prior to coming on board, Chad made an egg carved out of mahogany. It had a hollow center, which allowed all of us to write a little note to Heidi, fold it up, and put it inside. Chad then put the egg together and superglued the middle shut. With all the love notes inside, I took the egg and dropped it overboard into the Atlantic. It fell ten stories to the water below, and then it floated past. The scene was perfect. Other cruise ships were lit up close by. The sky was beautiful, the stars were plentiful, and the moon was shining brightly over the water. This was a beautiful tribute to a beautiful person.

—Same.

Chapter 28

There is No Fairy Dust

March 20, 2016, 8:36 p.m. (Day 201)

This has been a very heavy weekend. Yesterday, while going through Heidi's nightstand, I stumbled across some photos and cards, still in their envelopes. There was a picture of Heidi and me together at a restaurant. I don't know when it was, but it must have been a while ago, based on the darkness of my hair. We looked really happy. Then there were three pictures of Heidi in her hospital bed when she had Madeline, and a picture of Madeline when we were leaving the hospital after she was born. The date on the back was December 2001. These images are a far cry from the images of Heidi in the hospital last year that have been plaguing me. These were much happier times.

There was a card she wrote to me for our ninth anniversary, and another for my thirty-ninth birthday and another for either a birthday or anniversary.

Finding these cards took the wind right out of me, and I have not recovered since. In fact, I'm shedding more tears just reading them again and writing about them in this post. It's so hard to come across memories of happier times and then look up and see my empty room.

March 25, 2016, 8:01 a.m. (Day 206)

Finding the cards that Heidi wrote has affected my entire week. It was an emotional moment that I haven't completely moved past. As long as I've stayed busy, I've been able to maintain myself. In calmer moments, my mind has wandered. Just yesterday, while driving to an appointment for work, I heard "Never Surrender" by Corey Hart, and the waterworks flowed. I've heard this song a lot, and every time I hear it, I think of Heidi; for me that was her fight song.

March 31, 2016, 9:03 a.m. (Day 212)

Today is March 31, 2016. Seven months ago my life changed forever. I was thrust into this new life I didn't want and didn't ask for. Reflections, thoughts, memories. It's a path no one can help me navigate: not friends, not family, not even my kids.

Many have told me how strong they think I am and what an amazing job I have done adjusting to my new life. I don't feel strong. I don't feel amazing. I feel like I am held together by duct tape and bubblegum, at any moment I might separate into pieces. Every day I wake up and put on my armor. This allows me to get through the day, to work and function. My outward appearance is of strength and stability. When I remove the armor in the quiet places by myself, an entirely different person emerges—a person who just wants to get past today and get to tomorrow, frustrated with being by himself and tired of changing and adjusting.

April 11, 2016, 9:00 p.m. (Day 223)

My annual eye exam. Every year my eye doctor tells me that my eyesight, like my age, is one year older. Like every year, today I expected to be told the prescription for my contacts needs to get a little stronger and the number on my reading glasses has gone up a little. What I was not ready for was what happened when I arrived.

Every year, the receptionist pulls out a personal information sheet and asks me to review it and make changes, if any. Usually, there are no changes, but today there was one big change. The last time I was here was April 2015. I looked over the sheet and noticed the marital status section. I had the *M* circled. Next to it were other choices: *S, D,* and *W.* The dreaded *W.* This is the scarlet letter I now wear. I crossed out the *M* and circled the *W.*

It didn't stop there. Once in the exam room, the doctor came in and started his annual check-in conversation. How is business, how is the family, anything new? Anything new? Since last April? Unfortunately, something very new. I proceeded to tell him about Heidi's passing, and this look of shock overcame him. He had also been her optometrist for many years. He'd had no idea. He was dumbfounded. He didn't know what to say. Fighting back the tears, I told him the story. It was a hard story to hear and to tell. He told me what a loss to the world this was, that she was an amazing person, the likes of which people do not come across very often.

April 25, 2016, 12:09 p.m. (Day 237)

"Happy Anniversary." These are two words I think get taken for granted. They are said sometimes out of routine and sometimes out of obligation. On this day seventeen years ago, Heidi and I were married. Every year after, we would wish each other a happy anniversary. I would go to the store and spend time in the card section, one of my least favorite things to do, looking for just the right card that had just the right saying on it to represent our marriage in that moment. Every year on our anniversary we would exchange cards, and we would read the little extra messages we wrote to each other. We'd continue the celebration with a nice dinner, at a more expensive restaurant than we would usually dine at. This was our ritual for sixteen years, and we loved it. Even last year, while Heidi was in the middle of her chemo treatments, we were able to get out and have a wonderful dinner and be grateful for the opportunity to spend another anniversary together.

This year is different. I cannot say to her "Happy Anniversary." There is nothing happy about it. No one says, "Sad Anniversary."

I have come to the cemetery to spend time with Heidi and recognize this day for what it is: a day to celebrate the sixteen years we were blessed to have with each other. I've come to spend time with Heidi the only way I'm now allowed to. Sitting on top of her gravesite is the only physical connection I can have with her. Today we will not be able to exchange cards explaining how much we love each other and how grateful we are to be together. However, I still got her one and left it with her.

Tonight we won't be able to go out to a nice restaurant, just the two of us, and enjoy a great meal. So although I cannot, with integrity and honesty, say to Heidi "Happy Anniversary," today is still a very important day in our lives and in mine. It's a day and a date that will ALWAYS belong to the two of us. Today would have been seventeen years of marriage. Not one of them was ever a year I was unhappy or living in regret.

May 7, 2016, 7:36 p.m. (Day 249)

Today, we moved into a new home.

Our landlord had refused to renew our lease as he was planning to sell the house, so for the past two months, I have been preparing for this move. Although he reached out to me at the eleventh hour to offer a lease extension, I politely turned him down. My reason had become clear: in order for us to move forward, we had to move out.

In our garage were countless boxes from when Heidi first moved to Arizona back in 1992, still sealed and labeled with a red *H*. Four file cabinets were filled to overflowing with copies of every letter or card Heidi had ever sent. She had her undergraduate thesis paper and three of her friends' thesis papers. There was a multitude of folders filled with articles she had written and examples of resumes she liked. The cabinets contained twenty years of tax returns and all the original documentation that accompanied them. She maintained files on everybody, just like the FBI. She had a file on Chad, one on her father, and one for each of the kids.

After going through the file cabinets, Judy and I opened the H boxes. Inside, we found what appeared to be every piece of artwork Heidi had ever made, writing samples, old clothing, childhood toys, and memorabilia from every relative she ever came in contact with. Judy and I were shocked at what Heidi had kept.

On several occasions, Jack had told me he was eager to move. When I asked him why, he repeated the same answer, "Because there are no good memories here." He was right. While living in this house we experienced the passing of Heidi's father, Ira, and then Heidi's diagnosis, and eventually her passing. Shadows of Heidi were everywhere: at the vanity in the bathroom applying her makeup, at her desk researching information for one of the children's school projects, in the garage getting wrapping paper to wrap a gift to take to a birthday party, and sitting at the table asking everyone about their day over dinner. When I sat in the family room I saw dozens of people gathered for Heidi's shiva; when I went to bed I saw her propped up with no fewer than seven pillows for support, battling extreme nausea and trying to hydrate herself with any liquid she could. We couldn't stay.

Our new home is different in a number of ways. For one thing, it's a two-story house, something Heidi never would have agreed to; stairs aggravated her knees. The kitchen is average in size, and the pantry is small—although large enough to accommodate my limited abilities as a cook and baker. There's a pool in the backyard, and upstairs, everyone has his or her own bedroom. My parents even got their guest room back. The kids and I are happy with our choice.

May 8, 2016, 11:45 a.m. (Day 250)

Mother's Day is a day when Mom is celebrated. It's a day to overpay for breakfast and give Mom flowers. Today my kids woke up and they had no mother to celebrate.

The obvious plan was to take the kids to the cemetery. Of course, Madeline didn't want to go. She's still struggling with the reality of this loss.

The day started out as I had anticipated. We awoke to a heaviness in the house. I could see grief on the faces of my children. I reminded them that I wanted us to go see their mother. The boys agreed, but Madeline shook her head. She wasn't interested in going; she couldn't go. I told Madeline she needed to go, that it was the right thing to do. There were only two days a year she should see her mother: today and August 1, Heidi's birthday. The more I urged, the further into despair Madeline retreated. I was surprised by her resistance. She has been in therapy to work through these feelings, and I thought by now she'd be ready to face the cemetery. I wasn't sure what to do. I didn't want to push Madeline to do something she was clearly not comfortable with, but I also felt strongly that she needed to see her mother. If she kept avoiding these visitations, they would never get easier.

At a standstill with how to handle the conflict between my wishes and Madeline's feelings, I called a friend who had lost her mother at a young age, requesting her guidance. My friend told me that when she was a young girl, she wasn't ready to come face to face with seeing her mother's resting place and headstone; it was still too much for her to take in. Yet, she was forced to go and pay her respects. This traumatized her and created a negative association with going to the cemetery. As she grew older, she stopped going and hasn't been back in years.

I was grateful for my friend's input. It made me think carefully about how I was handling this situation with Madeline. I felt she needed to go, but it was clear she felt differently; she didn't share my sense of obligation. I had to remind myself that everyone's grief journey is unique. I told Madeline, "I think it would be good if you went to the cemetery, but if you don't want to go, I won't force you." I saw the sense of relief on her face.

Shortly after my conversation with Madeline, the boys and I left for the cemetery. We parked and walked down the concrete aisle toward Heidi's gravesite.

Upon our arrival, my children changed. There was a silence among them. Nobody spoke, nobody argued, and nobody annoyed each other. This was a moment between my kids and their mother. One of sadness and reflection.

Visiting Heidi is like stepping into a time machine; when I arrive, I cannot look away from the date on the plate on her stone: August 31,

2015. I'm transported back to that day every time I look at it. The day time stopped for her.

Going to the cemetery to see Heidi has never been easy. Every time I go, I experience it differently. Sometimes I am overtaken with grief and sadness; other times I feel a connection with her that brings me some level of comfort. The one thing that stands true is that every time, it's emotional.

The boys were quiet and stoic. Jack sat on a bench across from Heidi and next to his grandfather's grave, punching holes in a leaf with a small twig, like the holes in his heart. Max was standing next to me, cuddled under my arm. I glanced down at him and saw a tear running down his face. We didn't have to stay long to feel the moment.

As we were leaving, Jack told me about all the Mother's Day posts flooding social media. Everywhere he looked was "Happy Mother's Day." He said, "I want to take a selfie with mom's grave behind me in the background and post '#greatestmothersdayever.'"

Later that evening, Max had a flag football game. When it started, Max's head was somewhere else. He complained he wasn't getting enough playing time from his coach, who was only putting him in on defense. His body language was pouty, and he didn't look ready to play. His arms hung so low, he looked like a gorilla dragging his knuckles across the ground. If I had been his coach, I would have benched him as well. To add fuel to the fire, they lost the game. Afterward, the team huddled around the coach to cheer and show their sportsmanship. They all put their hands in a circle and shouted "MOMS!" on three. Hearing that was the straw that broke my little boy's back. In an instant, he turned to me and stuffed his head into that space between my shoulder and ribs and cried.

Back at home, Madeline had spent her Mother's Day looking at family photos on Heidi's Instagram and phone.

Although I share the grief of Heidi's loss with my children, I cannot imagine their pain. What it is like to be a fourteen-year-old girl and not have a mother to share girl stuff with, or to be a momma's boy without a momma. I feel helpless in my abilities to take away their sadness and make everything better, to fill the void in their lives.

For these three young kids, there can be no happy Mother's Day.

May 12, 2016, 9:44 p.m. (Day 254)

Since the move, Max has been concerned with one major decision at the new house. He asks me frequently where are we going to put the pictures of Heidi we had displayed in our old house above the fireplace. I haven't stumbled across the solution to Max's concern just yet. I've been preoccupied with where all the boxes in the garage will go, so I can move my car in. And where the pillowcases for my pillows disappeared to and how three boxes of bathroom items will fit into three drawers in the bathroom. I guess I had bigger things to figure out instead of where some pictures will go. For Max, I believe there is no bigger thing to figure out.

Tonight after our grief counseling session, Max showed me the picture frame he constructed in his group. He decorated the frame with two cancer ribbons, and in the middle where the picture would go, he wrote: "In memory of Heidi."

Designing this picture frame clearly stirred something within him. On the ride home he had been very quiet, and when we got back to the house, he'd asked me to come upstairs so he could show me something. In my room, he came to me with the frame, wrapped his arms around me, and began to cry.

Because my kids seem so put together and outwardly managing this loss remarkably well, I sometimes lose track of the harsh reality for them that lies just below the surface. It's hard to see my children in these moments. I want to wave that parental magic wand and make everything better, but I know I can't. There is no fairy dust I can throw to give them their mother back. I can only hug my kids and let them cry, and let them know that it is okay to be sad and to miss her. I can only reassure Max that we will add a photo and find a spot in our new home for the picture frame he designed out of love.

May 22, 2016, 8:14 a.m. (Day 264)

I should have known better. I sit here wiping tears from my face. I needed to get a note from Heidi's phone. I looked through a few boxes, but couldn't find it. After a brief panic, it appeared. Of course, there was no power, so I plugged it in and waited for it to come alive. I looked through the seemingly millions of notes that she kept on her phone and couldn't find what I was looking for. Then, for some reason, I went to her text messages. There were several dated August 30, 2015, the day before she passed away. As I read these messages, I could feel her flowing through me. I could picture her so vividly sitting up in bed, typing the responses to her friends who were texting her that night. "Falling asleep here. I better go. Have a good night. . . . Okay, we can talk tomorrow." Then the next day texts came in from those who had not known yet. "Are you doing ok today? I've been worried about you!" 12:49 p.m. "How R U doing?" 10:21 a.m.

I am so grateful to have these texts, but every time I see them they overwhelm me. Thank god for her phone. There is so much life in that phone. That phone holds her soul.

May 26, 2016, 11:20 a.m. (Day 268)

Congratulations to Madeline. Today was her moving-up ceremony marking her transition out of middle school and into high school.

It was a typical ceremony. There was no parking, even if you got there early. Parents were funneled in through the gate by the hundreds, and there was not enough seating to accommodate all in attendance. Madeline told me this day was not a big deal, and I think she is more excited about going to the water park later today with her friends then she was about graduating eighth grade. I have to admit I fed into her "take it or leave it" attitude, until I arrived. Everywhere I looked, there were sets of proud parents caught up in the moment. Moms and dads grinning widely. It was hard to make the walk toward the gym being only a dad.

When I arrived in the gym we were packed into the bleachers like sardines. It became standing room only. Then in came Madeline marching with her class to her seat. I'm not a big picture taker, but I tried to capture what I could. As I watched this procession I started to cry. What an amazing moment, which Heidi would have loved to see. I heard her in my head telling me what a proud mama she was.

It is one thing to talk about all the events Heidi will miss, it's another to be at them without her. Today was the first of many graduations Heidi will be unable to attend. I am very proud of my new high school freshman.

Chapter 29

The Shadow

June 10, 2016, 6:15 p.m. (Day 283)

The shadow has been following me around all day. Grief decided to come visit me again today. Nothing happened, nothing sparked it. It was just Friday. It was attached to me like skin. It affected my mood, it affected my work, it had complete control over me, and there was nothing I could do to shake it off. My office went out for a happy hour to celebrate a big closing, and I couldn't join them. I couldn't find enough light through the darkness. There was no explanation, it just was.

After work the shadow got me. I went to fill up the car with gas, and right after that the tears that had been fighting to come out all day finally arrived. I needed that release. Although I don't feel better, I at least feel less followed.

I am sending the kids out to dinner with Judy, and I'm going to escape into a movie by myself. I need some me time to recover. It's been a little over nine months, and it still stings. My feelings of grief and loss are always just below the surface, and on most days I can keep them there, but these feelings fight hard to be present and in control. The good news is that tomorrow is another day, and usually that means these moments of sadness go back into their bottle.

This is never easy!

June 25, 2016, 6:07 p.m. (Day 298)

This morning I woke up and did what I do on many mornings: I wrote a page of my story. What made this post worthy just took place a few minutes ago. Judy and I were out running an errand or two, and when we got back she mentioned a picture she saw earlier on Facebook. The picture was of me and two of my friends, Greg and Brad, with our newborn children. Most don't know this, but when Madeline was born, the three of us were delivering babies on the same day at the same hospital. My, Brad's, and Greg's kids all have the same birthday. Having my friends there with me made the experience of having a child even better. Brad's wife was in the room next door to Heidi, and Greg's wife down the hall. It was uncanny.

So why am I describing this moment and why does it matter? I am talking about it because this morning, when I was writing, I described the very moment this picture was taken, the moment when the three dads hung out in a hallway with our newborn babies on our laps. And then Judy mentioned the photo had been shared on Facebook.

Since Heidi's passing, my life has been filled with moments that are clearly not coincidental. I would like to think that maybe Heidi is giving me little hints that she is out there watching. I think she would approve of how we are doing.

July 16, 2016, 7:26 a.m. (Day 319)

Yesterday, I put the finishing touches on our trip to Hawaii in October. Having a trip to go on is giving me and the kids something to look forward to.

Over this past year the kids and I have done a lot of traveling. We've gone to Disneyland, taken a cruise, and explored San Francisco, and we're now looking toward Hawaii. These trips have been our salvation, bringing something positive to balance unimaginable loss. I've used these trips to trick our emotions through the grieving process. It has been my plan to give us something to look forward to every few months so we wouldn't just sit around focusing on the huge void we experience every day without Heidi.

I've discussed with my kids the very adult concept of life insurance. As an insurance agent myself for almost seventeen years, I never would have thought the most important policy I ever placed would be the one on Heidi. Heidi's passing was completely unexpected and sudden. She was not supposed to die at forty-eight and leave me and three young kids behind, but she did. Her policy has relieved some of the financial pressures I had. It has provided us the ability to create new and positive memories. I can't imagine what this year would have been like without that policy, not just because of the positive experiences it brought, but because of how it alleviated financial pressures from life's other stresses and loss.

This journey has reenergized me in my job as an insurance agent. I now have a goal to talk to as many people as I can about the benefits of having life insurance, through a story I wish I didn't have to tell. I couldn't change Heidi's diagnosis and eventual passing. I didn't have control over that. I did have control over the decision to carry and maintain a life insurance policy on Heidi, even when it might have made financial sense to remove the cost of it. Heidi's passing and the policy she had are two things that have changed my life forever, one negative and one positive.

August 1, 2016, 8:35 p.m. (Day 334)

Today would have been Heidi's forty-ninth birthday. It has been a very somber day. We cannot find the energy to celebrate since we can't celebrate with her; all we can do is recognize it for what it is. We can remember who she was and how she lived.

Today Judy, the kids, and I went to the cemetery and placed rocks on her newly placed headstone, giving her a hug. We released balloons into the air, as if to decorate her room as she would have decorated the kids' rooms. I brought home a cookie cake, her favorite; with every bite I could see and hear Heidi enjoying her birthdays of past.

Today also opens the door to August, the month I've been dreading for a year. I have made many strides, but these next few steps are the steps I fear the most. In addition to her birthday, this month I will face Jack's bar mitzvah without his mother, the official unveiling of Heidi's gravestone (complete with epitaph), and the anniversary of her death. All these events combined into one month seem like more than I can handle.

Two days ago, as Jack was getting excited for his birthday and about becoming a teenager, he described his memories of his birthday a year ago and where we were and what we were doing. He then told me how long ago it seemed, how far away his last birthday felt. He remarked that he almost didn't remember what it felt like to have a mom or a second parent. As we get older, time holds less of an impact. When you are thirteen, a year can seem to last a lifetime.

August 19, 2016, 8:40 a.m. (Day 352)

As I find myself getting closer to the anniversary of Heidi's death I am overtaken with emotions. For several days, and more strongly today, my thoughts go in and out like the tide. When I am busy with the kids or with work, I am focused on the task at hand. When I have a free moment, my thoughts wander to one year ago.

At this time last year I was managing twenty-three pills a day for Heidi. She was in the middle of the supplemental two-week chemo treatment and was getting sicker, but it was, at the time, "cancer as usual," as it had been for eight months.

Memories of our life before cancer seem so distant. We built eighteen years of memories, yet cancer has overtaken those as well.

I am putting together the last-minute touches on Jack's bar mitzvah for next weekend, and I am constantly aware of Heidi's absence. I compare Jack's upcoming celebration to Madeline's a year and a half ago. I don't compare the service or the party or even the events themselves. What I can't get out of my head is having Heidi at Madeline's and not at Jack's. It is such a horribly strange difference, and I cannot escape it. And it makes me so sad for Jack. For all of us.

August 24, 2016, 6:29 a.m. (Day 357)

As the big date nears, I find myself back in the fog that engulfed me when Heidi died. I haven't felt this way for almost a year now. It's hard to focus at work and I am tired throughout the day, regardless of how much I've slept.

However, what I find to be most fascinating is the relationship I now have with my emotions. I recognize that these are not just random feelings taking over my psyche, but a way of connecting with Heidi. I cannot hold her or touch her or laugh with her; I can only be with her through how I feel. I miss her terribly, and it's hard to remain in that emotional state for an extended period of time, yet I welcome the sadness and the emotions. I'm grateful to feel them and have them be present in my life, because it is through these emotions that I'm in touch with who I was, and through them Heidi and I will remain together.

August 29, 2016, 6:37 a.m. (Day 363)

August 27 was the date Heidi and I had chosen back when Jack was ten, in consultation with our rabbi, for Jack's bar mitzvah. We left that appointment excited and eager to see Jack's special day unfold.

But now, how was I to balance Jack's celebration with the anniversary of the worst day in my life—in all our lives? I had little faith in my ability to pull that off, so I approached our rabbi and asked if there was anything that could be done to move Jack's ceremony. Dates were routinely booked years in advance; it couldn't be moved. To complicate things more, we hadn't yet held the unveiling of Heidi's headstone, which is a ceremony normally done around the one-year anniversary of a death. I scheduled Heidi's unveiling for the Monday after Jack's celebration. It made sense to do it then so that family already in town could attend the ceremony.

When we entered August and his date drew nearer, Jack came to me and asked for my assurance that the anniversary of Heidi's death would not overpower his celebration. His request raised the bar.

The date was set, but the planning was just beginning. Thankfully,

Jack chose to have a celebratory trip, rather than a huge, extravagant party like his sister. Nonetheless, friends and family would be in town, and we needed to do something to celebrate with them. Heidi had loved this sort of thing, but party planning was not in my DNA. I couldn't spend hours online researching colors or themes, as Heidi did. I wanted Jack to have a great time, but I had no creative talent to pull out all the stops. With Judy by my side, I embarked on a journey to make a memorable event for my son.

At the end of August in Scottsdale, the options for a celebration are limited. My vision was to have a small party that would be shared with family and friends, but because of the extreme heat, any event would have to be held inside. On the one hand, I didn't want to spend the money on a hotel party; on the other, I didn't want to have Jack's bar mitzvah at a bowling alley. My choices were limited. A friend suggested I contact a nearby aquatic center managed by the city of Scottsdale. As luck would have it, the facility was available for rent after hours. For $1,500 I could have the place to ourselves from 6:00 to 9:00 p.m. What a place this was! It had an eight-lane, twenty-five-yard lap pool; four diving boards at various heights; a three-story water slide, lazy river, and shallow play pool; water features, a spray pad, and veranda seating. This was exactly what I was looking for. So this is what we did.

I hired a DJ to keep the party going with music. I catered Mexican food and bought blue tablecloths to dress up the eating area. On each table, I filled two glass bowls with Jack's favorite candy. I did my best to mimic Heidi's attention to detail and make it a fantastic event for Jack.

The party was planned, but I still had to face getting through the weekend emotionally intact. I had to somehow be present for Jack and allow him his moment of celebration and also address the huge void created by Heidi's absence that would place a shadow over everything.

Family started to arrive from all over the country the Wednesday before the bar mitzvah. Friday night, Jack stepped into his role as the bar mitzvah boy, leading prayers throughout that evening's Shabbat service. Afterward, family and out-of-town guests retreated to a private room I had booked at one of our favorite Italian restaurants. Upon arrival, guests were served drinks, and everyone began to help themselves to the pizza, pasta, and salad buffet. The guests looked happy as relatives caught up with each other after long absences. Everyone was enjoying themselves—except me. I moved around the room playing host and involved myself in the conversations as best I could, but I didn't feel the joy of the moment. I was wearing my "everything is all right" mask, but underneath I couldn't escape the loneliness I felt experiencing this important occasion by myself, as I thought about how Heidi would have loved it. The weekend was just beginning, and I was already struggling.

The following morning, I put on my suit and prepared to see my son transition from boy to man. Jack did a wonderful job at his bar mitzvah service. He hit every note and recited every prayer with conviction; the eight months of practice and religious learning had paid off.

As I stood in front of the congregation to give the speech praising Jack, I was speaking for two. Everyone in the audience who knew and loved Heidi would be waiting for me to acknowledge her absence and release the tension. This would be the most important speech of my life. The time had come. I stood next to my son, looked at him and then at the audience, took a deep breath, and began.

When I finished, I again looked at the audience. Many were wiping tears from their cheeks. As I walked back to my seat, the room felt different. My speech had acknowledged everyone's grief over losing Heidi, and then released it. Heidi's absence was addressed and given value; we all now had permission to move on with the celebration.

At 6:00 the guests began to arrive at the aquatic center. Jack was in the pool with his friends, Max was jumping off diving boards, and Madeline was riding the waterslide. Music filled the air, and I had a smile on my face that felt like a smile. As the sun set, adults and kids alike gathered in the pool, and a chair was brought in. Jack sat on the chair and in an instant was lifted out of the water. The DJ was playing the music to the "Hora," the traditional circle dance at Jewish weddings and bar mitzvahs to recognize those being celebrated. In what I believed to be the first water "Hora" ever, Jack was lifted and surrounded by friends and family. When the music stopped, Jack was flipped backward, feet over head, into the water.

Unlike the night before, I didn't need my "everything is all right" mask; everything was all right. In fact, it was better than all right. Everyone was having a wonderful time.

As the weekend came to a close, I looked back at the events and felt pleased. The months of nervous anxiety over blending loss and celebration were now behind me; I had pulled it off. Jack had his celebration, and Heidi had her recognition. The balance I had feared was impossible had become another sign of my own inner strength and my ability to continue to find my way in a world without Heidi.

Chapter 30

A Woman of Valor

August 29, 2016, 8:03 p.m. (Day 363)

Today was the unveiling of Heidi's headstone. This was an event I have been anticipating for quite some time now. It's a short service of remembrance conducted graveside. Our immediate family gathered, joined by others who were still in town for Jack's bar mitzvah a few days ago. Additionally, I invited the eight women who were the pallbearers at Heidi's funeral. All attended.

At the beginning of the ceremony, the headstone is covered. By the end, it is uncovered. It is said that prior to this ceremony the spirit is present and hovers around our world and always close by. Once the headstone is uncovered, the spirit is released and allowed to rise and rest in peace. The spirit is given freedom to move on, and those left behind are given the freedom to move on as well. It is a beautiful tradition.

Moving on does not mean to forget or dismiss; it's just a release, an end of mourning and a new beginning, one that looks toward the future and is at peace with the past. Heidi has touched and changed my soul, and that will never change.

As he had done at her funeral, the rabbi once again read the poem from the Bible that describes "A Woman of Valor." He mentioned that he has officiated at many funerals, but only on very few occasions is he compelled to recite this poem. For Heidi, the title, "A Woman of Valor," is a fitting tribute and is forever etched upon her gravestone.

A Woman of Valor
What a precious find is a woman of valor!
Her worth is far beyond rubies.
Her husband puts his confidence in her and lacks no good thing.
She is good to him, never bad, all the days of her life . . .
She opens her hand to the needy,
And extends her hand to the poor . . .
She is clothed with strength and splendor,
She looks to the future cheerfully.
She opens her mouth with wisdom;
Her tongue is guided by kindness.
She oversees the activities of her household
And never eats the bread of idleness.
Her children come forward and bless her,
Her husband praises her (and says):
"Many women have done superbly,
But you surpass them all."
Charm is deceitful and beauty—vain,
But a God-revering woman is much to be praised.
Extol her for the fruit of her hand,
Wherever people gather,
Her deeds speak her praise.
—Proverbs

This poem has affected me again today as it did the first time I heard it, so long ago. Never had I heard such a beautiful and accurate portrayal of the human being that Heidi was.

As the rabbi explained this morning, I hope we all find a new beginning and in that beginning we find ways to continue Heidi's legacy. Pick up the phone and call an old friend you haven't spoken to in forever. Volunteer your time or help someone in need. Do the right thing, even if the right thing is hard. Have dinner with your family and cherish that time. Go out into the world and create memories, because there may be a time when memories are all you have. Take wedding vows seriously, for better or for worse, in sickness and in health and till death do us part. Make your days count, and make a difference.

Heidi was the most amazing wife, mother, daughter, sister and friend that this world may ever know. I miss her daily, and I was blessed to have been able to share my life, for any amount of time, with her.

Heidi,

You will always hold a special place in our hearts where you can come forever. I love you so very, very much.

—Same

Chapter 31

Same to All

August 31, 2016, 8:59 a.m. (1 year)

The end of August completes the circle. We have all aged.

I cannot keep myself from looking at the time. In my head I'm reliving the events of a year ago, moment by moment and minute by minute. It is now 8:00; in 10 minutes I'll be rushing Max out the door to school, in approximately forty-five minutes I'll be on the phone with 911, and on the phone with Chad, telling him to get on a flight and "get here now!"

Within the next two hours, I'll be in a small hospital room inside the emergency room holding Heidi's hand and watching her take her last breath.

One year ago today, within the next two hours, it will be all over. No more managing medication, no more chemo treatments, no more watching Heidi be so sick, no more laughing, no more conversations, no more "us shows" on TV. I'll be looking at the beginning of my life without her in it.

Since dropping the kids at school this morning, I haven't been able to hold myself together. Once I was by myself I was unable to focus on anything else but the ticking clock. With every passing minute I am reintroduced to the memory of a moment. With every memory I am greeted with a stream of tears. I haven't cried like this in a long time. The memories of a year ago are raw and intense.

I am currently dysfunctional. I canceled my workout, and I can't go to the office. I am alone in my grief, and it is where I need to be. 8:28 . . . tick, tick, tick . . .

It was unclear how today would go. Living one day at a time has taught me not to predict tomorrow. After surviving the events of the past several days, the bar mitzvah and the unveiling, I thought that maybe today wouldn't be as bad as I originally anticipated. I was wrong, it is. However, today is a brand-new day, and with it comes its own agenda. Today is not easy. Today does not belong to the present, it belongs to the past.

8:58 . . . tick, tick, tick . . .

August 31, 2016, 10:38 a.m.

10:05 . . . It was all over now. I have sat here in my room this morning in silent vigil watching time. This time a year ago she was gone, and I would be searching for the strength to go and tell my children their mother had died.

Time will slow, and reality will change. This is what it's like to lose someone you love.

Today will be a day of reflection and living in the past. A year ago began life challenges that were unimaginable.

A lot has changed in a year. I have grown emotionally on a scale I couldn't have envisioned. I have become a writer, and Heidi is certainly chuckling about it. I have found positives rising like a Phoenix out of a horrific negative. I have grown as a person and as a father. I have found out what matters and what is important in my life. I have found strength where only weakness was present. I have learned to carry a kindred spirit with me wherever I go and to connect with that spirit in different ways. I have walked through darkness and come out the other side.

I have now completed a year of firsts, and I enter a lifetime of "anothers." Another holiday without Heidi, another anniversary, birthday, and Mother's Day without her. Another celebration, another vacation, another day.

Posting my story on Facebook in this public forum has saved my life. I don't know what state I would be in if I had not had this medium to express my feelings and get through the anguish. I am grateful for being able to see how many people like a post or comment on one. It truly helps. There's no easy way to get through a life-changing event such as this, but the support I've received has been the wind beneath my wings.

I don't know what tomorrow or next week or even next year will look like. What I do know is that I will continue to show up for my kids. I will continue to show up for myself, and I will continue to show up for Heidi.

—Same to all. . . .

Epilogue: Life Really Does Go On

On December 1, 2017, I turned fifty. A big birthday, a milestone, the start of a new decade. It was a day I'd hoped would feel different, like a celebration; it did. I arrived at my office in the morning to find a birthday card, signed by everyone. Next to the card on my desk was a large homemade brownie with the number "50" written out in M&Ms atop; I devoured it in just a few bites. My agenda for the day was full. I needed to pick up Jack early from school and get him to his endocrinologist for his quarterly checkup; diabetes doesn't care what day you're having. In the afternoon, Madeline would be dropped off at my office after school, and we would go get my newly sixteen-years-old daughter her driver's license. Her license was the best gift I was given—it was the gift of freedom. I no longer had to take her to a friend's house, the mall, Starbucks, or anywhere! My birthday was in high gear.

After work when I arrived home, the celebration continued. I walked through the garage door and straight into a party. My kitchen table was adorned with gifts, blowers, and party hats. I was soon instructed to go upstairs to my bedroom and "brush my hair" before leaving for the restaurant for dinner. Opening my bedroom door, I walked through a waterfall of streamers. There was a large banner on the wall wishing me a "Happy 50th Birthday," and below it on my bed were fifty balloons covering it like a comforter. Seeing that many balloons transformed me out of my current age and back to that of a child. Of course, I had to get a running start and belly flop into the middle of the bed. Balloons flew everywhere! I could hear the laughter from my children as I bounced, and then I looked up with mild embarrassment as I noticed they'd captured the entire event through video on their smartphone.

From the moment they planned it, the kids couldn't wait for me to come home and experience the celebration. At dinner, they excitedly told me which idea was drafted from which person and who picked out what items; they were beaming with pride. It was a competition between siblings, and I was the winner. This was how Heidi celebrated loved ones, and my children had internalized the ritual and made it their own. Heidi had a way of making everyone feel important on their special day. My children knew turning fifty was a big deal, and they made it as special as Heidi would have, in their own way.

I realized that I enjoyed the day, and that life, in fact, does go on.

Twice in One Lifetime

I spent almost three years grieving, posting, and writing. During that period, my children kept growing, and I kept moving forward. As I mentioned in my reflections on dating, I think it's not in my DNA to be alone. I knew it was only a matter of time until I found love again. But how does that happen? How do you move forward after the loss of the one person you believed you were meant to be with for the rest of your life? It's not easy. It takes effort–a lot of effort.

While writing this book, I decided to dip my feet into the dating pool with the hopes there was someone out there for me. I subscribed to four dating sites, created a profile, posed for some pictures, and went out into the world. I went on dozens of first dates, and each one seemed to be the same: nice conversation, no sparks, check please. My rapid transformation into the "king of first dates" was no surprise to me. I knew it would be a challenge for a woman to latch on when all I wanted to talk about was the book I was writing about my wife of 16 years who had recently passed away. Of course, I knew I was sabotaging my chances, but I couldn't help myself. At that time, the book was such a monumental part of my life that everything else came second. I continued to go on dates, each time telling myself, "Don't mention the book, don't mention the book." But always, I did.

After some time, a profile came across my path that intrigued me. It featured just one photo of a woman standing at the bottom of a staircase, so far away I had to zoom in to make out any of her features. The description was short and to the point as well, utilizing only one sentence to put a caption on the photo of her life. Adding to the mystery, her profile name was "Kotek," which made no sense to me at all.

Intrigued and feeling like I had nothing to lose, I swiped right and she responded. We texted back and forth and then three days later met for our first date. The plan was to arrive at 7:30. As I was walking to meet her, at 7:32, I received a text "are you coming?" Perhaps a second sentence on her profile highlighting punctuality would have been a benefit. Thankfully, I wasn't four minutes late or the date may have gone quite differently. When I arrived, she stood before me, and she was beautiful--far better looking than the photo of her 100 feet down on a staircase. I was excited and relieved. We sat down, ordered a few drinks and began to talk. Immediately I knew this date would be different from all the others. When she began to speak, she spoke with a Polish accent. The accent was a first for me; something new and endearing. She told me her name was Ewa (pronounced "Ava"). She also told me what Kotek meant. It's Polish for kitten. Mystery solved.

I had recently finished the first draft of the book, and of course, despite my better judgment, I started talking about it. This time it was different. Ewa didn't look to the exit for a quick getaway; she stayed, and we talked about her life, our children and other topics for hours. After almost a year of dating, finally, some chemistry! Within that first week, we saw each other three times, and we have been together ever since. In July of 2020, in the presence/company of our children, we exchanged vows along the beautiful beaches of Cancun, Mexico. Ewa is everything I was looking for; she checks all the boxes: She loves to wear heels, she loves bike riding and the outdoors, and most importantly she accepts my past and loves my children.

In order to move forward in one relationship I had to release another. I will always cherish my time with Heidi and look back on our years together with happiness. Heidi will always be the mother of my kids, and they will always miss her, but Ewa has brought a new happiness into all of our lives. Madeline now has another woman in her life in whom she can fulfill her desire for a motherly bond.

Moving forward in my new blended family hasn't been seamless, however. My new stepdaughter, Ewa's daughter Claudia, was born August 31st. Of course, August 31 is also the day Heidi died. When Ewa and I first got together I couldn't believe that of all the days in the calendar her daughter's birthday fell on that fateful day in my family's life. Each year, I struggle to balance these two occasions—one, a somber remembrance of a person and life that has passed; the other, a joyful celebration of an important member of my new family. As the years move forward, the grief in my life must change and adapt. Claudia's birthday reminds me that I will always walk a line where my past, present and future intersect.

For me, the grieving has subsided. I no longer feel like a walking wound. I still have vivid memories, but they no longer control me. When I think of Heidi now, I think of a happy family that was and a happy family that is again. I think of this incredible journey that has allowed me to become a writer and break through my grief and come out stronger. When I think of Heidi now, I think about how blessed I have been to be given the chance to find love and happiness twice in one lifetime.

Part Three

Takeaways

Introduction

While one of my motivations for writing this book was simply to tell the story of my love for Heidi, our relationship, and how I went on after losing her, sharing my story was only part of my purpose. The experience of navigating the loss of my wife and best friend was difficult and bewildering, to say the least. I thought if I could distill some of the lessons I learned through experience, it might help others who were at the beginning of their journeys.

In this section, I offer the most significant nuggets of wisdom I learned along the way, presented in a format that allows the reader to find what is most needed in a given moment in time. In short, I'm offering you what was in short supply for me in my grief—advice—in the hopes that at least some of it will be of benefit. Take what you like and leave the rest, as they say. If you're grieving, I hope some of these hard-won nuggets will offer reassurance.

Dealing with Loss

The Fog of Loss

The fog of Heidi's loss was overwhelming and all-encompassing, not unlike that deep fog that settles into the California Bay Area.

Just out of college, I moved to San Francisco and lived there for two years. On most mornings, a fog came in over the city. It was there when I woke up, and it took most of the morning to burn off. When I had to go to work, I had to drive through it. There are no barriers to keep it out, no walls to keep it back. When it arrives it covers everything. It hugs every corner, fills every space. There is a thickness about it; you can breathe it in, and it impairs your vision. You can feel it on your face and against your skin. The fog became a part of life.

Losing Heidi brought a fog like this into my life. It hugged every corner and filled every space, but was present only within myself.

When we lose someone we love, we need a coping mechanism in order to survive the intense pain of grief, so our brains create "the fog." It numbs your senses and slows everything down, leaving you in a dreamlike state. You walk without purpose, you show up without being present. You go through the daily motions of life, but you do it without care or concern. You're on autopilot. When you're in that liminal phase called grief, your real life seems far away; it seems outside of your reality. The fog buffers you from the real world.

The fog is powerful. It is all-encompassing; it takes over body and mind. The fog is the anesthesia the body needs to handle the trauma of grief. It fills the space in between the life you had and the new life you haven't quite adjusted to yet. It's desensitizing and makes you feel as if you're living in an alternate reality, but the world still moves forward. What's real is still real.

Throughout this period you may receive small reminders of the world you checked out of, tangible items that shock you out of the fog momentarily. Things you can touch and hold that transport you briefly back into reality and remind you that where you are is no dream.

There is no alarm that goes off to tell you your sentence is up. The fog will let you know when it is done with you, and as suddenly as it comes in, it will subside. Like anesthetic wearing off, your senses begin to come back. Time starts to move normally again, slowly but surely. Then one day, you wake up and discover that it's a new month. The fog is gone, though the grieving has only just begun.

Grief is a Rollercoaster

Going on a rollercoaster ride is about giving up control. When you step into that car, strap yourself in, and pull that bar over your head you accept whatever twists and turns await you and ready yourself for one wild ride. When it begins, you may feel your heart rate and blood pressure increase, your body may tense up, and you might be second-guessing your decision. You tell yourself that no matter what happens, it's not forever. You assure yourself you can get through this, and maybe you grab the hand of the person next to you for support. Ultimately, you allow yourself to release and enjoy the ride.

Grief is a rollercoaster. It locks you in, and it takes over control. But grieving is not fun, and it is certainly not a choice. Throughout my experience with grief I have observed different ways of coping and coming to terms with the new reality of loss. Some people return to work shortly after a loss in order to keep busy and distracted. Others live in denial and try to convince themselves that their loved one is on vacation or an extended business trip. Both of these approaches are attempts to attain a semblance of control, by choosing how you act and feel. But the control is an illusion. You can't kick this can down the road. Grief needs its moment; it demands recognition. Denial and distraction only postpone the inevitable. You cannot escape grief.

I believe that as human beings, we all have a primal fear of being out of control. We may experience the sensation of needing to grab hold of something secure when life feels out of control. But in times of grief there is nothing we can hold on to that will help us; quite the contrary, the only thing that can help us is to let go.

We try to control our lives and predict what will happen. We wear a watch so we can feel in control of time and plan our day. We use a calendar to plan our future. When we have children, we are already planning their path of education to help them get into a good college or get a good job. We want to control everything.

What happens when these decisions are taken away from us? When we realize that we can't control time or predict tomorrow? When we discover we are no longer in control of our emotions? When we realize we just can't have control over life? That moment becomes a fork in the road that demands a choice. If we react to the lack of control by fighting it, we'll likely feel worse, just a as rip current can drown you if you fight it. The only reasonable choice with grief is to somehow let go and let it carry you—accept it, give in, and move on.

Grief also presents us with baffling questions to which there are no answers. Why do we feel better one day, but on the very next day not feel better at all? After Heidi's death, time slowed so that minutes seemed like days. I lost control of my emotions. I could feel stable in the morning but completely distraught by the afternoon, crying uncontrollably, drenched in sadness and loneliness. I became unable to go anywhere without envisioning Heidi and me living our lives together. I saw her standing in the aisles grabbing groceries, sitting in a booth ordering lunch, and riding in the passenger seat as I drove down the road. Grief had me in a chokehold, and it wasn't letting go.

I came to recognize and accept that I was no longer in charge. Everything was different now; all I could do was strap myself in and go for the ride. I accepted that I wasn't in control of my emotions, or my present or my future. I was adrift, and I had to be okay with it.

Once I relinquished control, I began to live moment by moment. Nothing was predictable, and I could only experience the present. Because my future emotional status was uncertain, I stopped worrying about it. If I was sad, that was okay; if I wasn't sad, that was okay, too. When I was surrounded by emotional storm clouds and couldn't see any rays of sunlight, I told myself, *This is temporary. I can feel horrible now; tomorrow is another day.* And it always was. Releasing the pressure of maintaining control allowed me to move forward and heal.

Discovering how to live in the moment, to be present today and not worry about tomorrow, is one of the greatest gifts grief has given me. It's a way of living that I continue to incorporate into my life today. Grief still shows up, but when I experience moments of sadness, I'm able to embrace them and give them the attention they demand. I know this moment will pass, and tomorrow will be different. I can give up control, let go, and ride the rollercoaster. Like the ride, it's temporary, and when it's over, I will get off and move toward whatever is next in my life.

Grief Fades Over Time But It Brings Guilt

It's true. Grief fades over time. But along the way, as grief faded, it felt like I was slowly letting go of my memories of Heidi; as though Heidi were on the end of a rope, and I was desperately trying to hold on to it and keep her from dropping farther, but no matter how hard I grasped it, she kept slipping away. I wanted to remember. I needed to remember.

Within my grief I found myself able to remain close to Heidi, my memories vivid. When I cried and felt emotional, I was able to keep the rope from slipping; our spirits remained connected, and I felt her presence near me. I also held a strong sense of obligation to Heidi and my relationship with her, and grieving seemed to be the very least I could do to honor that relationship. It didn't feel like an honorable option to try to move on, to let go. Thus from trying to heal arose a new emotion —guilt.

My logical brain wanted to make sense of everything, and it told me what I thought grief should feel like. It wanted to impose order, rules, and societal expectations. My emotional brain didn't need to make sense at all. It just existed, and felt what it felt. Logically, I should not have felt any better just three weeks after Heidi's death. But emotionally, I *did* feel better, if even for a brief moment. The logical brain judged this as wrong.

Thus grief became my new relationship, my comfort, my anti-guilt. And I found myself living a conflict. Grieving was hard and exhausting; it hindered my ability to move forward, and it dominated everything I did.

I understand why young children cry when they lose their favorite stuffed animal or that physical something that connects them to comfort and security—their "wubby." Letting go of my grief "wubby" was hard.

I had to fight hard to accept that there was nothing wrong with me for feeling better. But once I did, as the days passed, my grief softened, and it became smaller and more manageable. I wanted to not be in pain anymore, even as I was conflicted and guilty about moving forward.

At that time, it felt like getting on with my life meant losing touch with my memories, and thus with all that was left of Heidi. The problem was, living in grief was not healthy, and I suspected that the comfort created by this connection to memory might become debilitating over time. I had to give myself permission to put my grief behind me once and for all in order to step out of my past and leap, or perhaps crawl, forward into my future. Transitioning through that moment marked the birth of my new life. And now I see grief for what it is: a necessary part of the healing process, but one we can embrace and then let go.

I can feel the distance I have traveled from my old life, my life with Heidi. The intensity of feelings behind the memories have faded some, and yet I still grieve, even four years later. The feelings of loss still arrive, and in certain moments I still connect with Heidi, but these moments don't carry the almost unbearable weight they once did. They also don't bring me the comfort they once did; they simply have become a part of my life. I have discovered that I can move forward and still retain the memories of the past—with sadness, sure, but without the conflict or guilt of letting go.

Navigating Grief as a Male

Society traditionally has scorned the value of showing emotion in men. To this I say, "To hell with society." Throughout my healing journey, my emotions were understandably unstable; at any given moment I could find myself overtaken with grief. This didn't always happen in private, where I could express myself and allow the emotions to run their course. When I was standing at Disneyland with my children watching the fireworks and sobbing uncontrollably, I was self-conscious that others were seeing me and judging me. I continuously wiped the tears off my face in an attempt to appear differently, yet the emotions of that moment were so intense that there was nothing I could do to hide them.

Unfortunately, we live in a society where it is socially unacceptable to air private emotions publicly, especially for men. I couldn't cry in the checkout line buying groceries without getting looks of confusion and perhaps annoyance from my fellow shoppers, or at least that's how it seemed to me. Those of us who are grieving live in a different world from those around us; we walk the same streets, but we travel a different path. In order to sustain my outward appearance and coexist with those who were not grieving, I developed a coping mechanism to hide my emotions. What I found was my "everything is all right" mask, at least in the early stages of grieving. To the world I looked as though I were improving, but privately I was not.

I believe people are genuinely good and want to do the right thing but don't always know how to. I imagine my situation made others uncomfortable because they hadn't experienced the grief that I had, and they didn't know how to react when they saw it. I don't expect the world to change or people to go out of their way to accommodate my feelings. It is my choice to live in the world with others, not the choice of others to live in mine. I was careful to not appear publicly as the grieving widower and create a space where people needed to walk on eggshells around me.

Still, it's important to find one's own way through grief and to have someone understand, someplace where you can remove the mask. It's crucial for you to find a way to acknowledge and accept what you are feeling. For me, I found it in a couple of close friends, the support of religious leaders, a therapy group, and Facebook, which allowed me to be myself to a safe audience.

Let me say that I have never considered myself to be a very religious person or even a very spiritual one. I'm not a regular at weekly services or even the High Holidays, Rosh Hashanah and Yom Kippur. I grew up proud of my religion and my heritage, but my connection always felt more cultural than observant. Yet I found that during my times of deepest grief, there was a comfort in being connected to my religious community.

Whether there is a family member, or a therapist, or peer counseling, or even a religious person to help, find that help, especially if you are wearing your "everything is all right" mask. Community, church, synagogue, or even posting on social media, as I did, can all bring great comfort, and help you through healing.

In the Role of Grieving Spouse, You Become a Bridge for Others

When you are the person closest to the departed loved one, friends want to touch you and speak with you in order to feel better about their own grief. Within the first few months after Heidi's passing, upon meeting someone in the grocery store, a sporting event, or while dropping off one of the kids, I found myself in a bit of an awkward situation. Once eye contact was made, I would be approached, hugged, and usually looked at with a slightly tilted head and wide eyes. On the surface these interactions appeared to be genuine and directed toward me, but over time it felt as though I became the substitute physical connection to Heidi. The hug with me became the hug with Heidi; the brief conversation with me became a conversation with Heidi.

These situations and interactions connect us all as human beings. If we live long enough, we will all lose someone we love, and if we are brave enough, we can acknowledge our frailty and grief with one another even when we don't really know each other. It's excruciating, yet it's also what humanizes us. Walking this path requires a constant juggle between your own grief and the grief of others. When those paths meet in the middle, whose grief wins? Perhaps there is no winner, but rather, there is a sharing of similar emotions, like two negatives making a positive. Perhaps it's our common need to connect and support others that gets us through the tough moments.

Special Occasions

Face it, they suck. Birthdays, anniversaries, holidays . . . the challenge is to learn to enjoy them again, to allow oneself to do so. Since losing Heidi I've become aware that there is a difference between having a birthday, for which I am grateful, and having a happy birthday, which, for a grieving person, can feel like a tall order.

Throughout the first year after Heidi's passing, I was vividly aware of being alone in group situations. I would watch other couples interact, finish each other's sentences, and maybe even bicker a little. On the outside I did my best to laugh, have great conversations, and enjoy myself, but just below the surface remained a lonely feeling of being without my plus-one.

Holidays and special occasions are about traditions, same foods, same company; allowing what you did last year to dictate what you do this year. For a grieving person, traditions are hard and represent tangible reminders of what is no longer. Moving forward requires traditions to be changed or adjusted. When the kids and I went to Disneyland a month and a half after Heidi's passing, our tradition of taking the train to Toontown and making "It's a Small World" our first ride changed. We were all aware that this is what we had done every time before, but this time, it felt okay, and perhaps necessary, to do something different. Thanksgiving 2017, my second without Heidi, saw my home host my two sisters and their families plus my parents—fourteen people in all. The boys went fishing with my dad, and Madeline braved the malls with me on Black Friday. A totally different crowd and a different direction; a dramatic change from Thanksgiving in the past.

As the years have passed, I've learned that it is okay to honor the holidays that were hers and ours without losing myself to overwhelming grief. I've also learned how to begin to create new holidays and new memories, and that it is okay to do so.

Healing is a Process

As I moved through grief, good days were not a given. I fought hard for them, and moving forward took tremendous effort daily, sometimes even hourly. I was emotionally fragile and could easily be derailed with the slightest wind.

Healing was and is a process. There were moments when grief released me and I could experience feeling happy again. It was energizing. When that happened, I believed I was making progress, and I wanted to keep moving forward. But these moments were sometimes short-lived. Eventually, something would trigger me: a memory, an encounter, a holiday, a task. These triggers brought my grief back to the surface. Suddenly I felt like I had been thrown into a place where my grief was heavier, more intense. It felt like I had regressed. These setbacks had me questioning my stability.

I came to learn, however, that feeling grief was not moving backward; it was simply part of the recovery process, and what felt like a reversal actually moved me forward in a "one step backward, two steps forward" way. My trip to Disneyland illustrated this. Prior to leaving, there were days when I felt better, as though I could actually look forward to something. I felt like I was moving on with my life and experiencing some happiness. Once at Disneyland, though, everyone around me seemed happy, I was overwhelmed with memories, and I struggled to drum up even a glimmer of cheerfulness. Truth be told, I allowed myself to wallow.

Looking back, I also see that my mind used my feelings to trick me. I was already in pain, and my mind told me stories that made me feel worse, like "I'm the only person at Disneyland feeling miserable," or "Disneyland set me back a mile; it impeded my growth and interfered with my healing." I realize now that that experience wasn't a setback at all, despite how it felt at the time. There's a perception that only happy or positive feelings can help to heal and move you forward, or that they indicate growth. We don't want to accept that unpleasant emotions are a part of the process. Getting through grief is not gradual and steady; it's not like walking up stairs, where each step gets you a little bit closer to the top. You don't get a little happier and better each day until you're magically healed. Grief doesn't work that way. Feeling good one day is no precursor to feeling good the next. Emotional waves arrive without warning. We have no choice but to ride them.

I learned a lot from that trip. I learned that I could come face to face with intense sadness and not let it destroy me. I also learned what I needed to do to make traveling happier in the future, and how to enjoy time with my children without Heidi. When the kids and I went on our next vacation, the cruise, I drew upon my Disneyland experience to realize that I could no longer hide behind grief or wallow in it. Nor did I need to out of a sense of loyalty to Heidi. It would have been easy to mope around, thinking "Heidi would've loved this. I wish she were here. It's not fair that I get to go on this trip and she doesn't." I had to consciously choose to allow myself happiness and enjoyment, no guilt. The cruise became a turning point in my grief journey, a symbol of experiencing life after Heidi in a positive way and a chance to learn how to cherish time with my children and to grow as a human being.

Heidi had gifted us the opportunity to travel and to establish a new, healthy lifestyle, and I knew she would be proud of us for not squandering it. Ironically, in the process of recreating our lives, I found myself grow closer to Heidi, not farther from her as I'd feared, because what she wanted for us in life, she gave to us in death. Our new start was her legacy.

Sometimes, condolences made me feel a setback. When people found out about Heidi, they inevitably offered some statement such as, "My condolences," or "I'm sorry." Every time this happened it created awkward moments, and it still does today. When I'm conversing with someone and Heidi's passing comes up, there is always an interruption. "I'm so sorry," the person says. And then, of course, I thank them. At that moment we resort to our societal training, like robots. Offering words of condolence to a stranger is a social construct. It's the polite thing to do, but the underlying truth is that it makes both parties feel uncomfortable, and for the one grieving, it immediately recalls the loss. As I've moved through the grief process, I now understand that recalling the loss will always be there, but it's okay to acknowledge it, say a silent prayer if that helps you, and move on with life.

Words to Comfort Those Who Are Grieving

As I mentioned above, the societal "I'm sorry" is a well-intentioned cultural response to learning of another's loss. We've all been conditioned to deal with feelings privately, and most of us have no idea how to confront emotional situations in public when we encounter them. When I tell someone "I lost my wife," I am sharing something deeply personal. My situation brings them close to their own fears of loss. Losing someone we love is unavoidable, whether it's a parent, grandparent, or spouse or a child. One day, we will all face our own journey of grief and loss. These interactions are uncomfortable because we know that someday we ourselves will be that grieving person.

I recognized the relative sincerity of "I'm sorry" from friends and relatives, as well as even from strangers. But each such encounter was awkward because it required a "thank you" from me, and in that moment, being thankful felt odd. What was I thanking them for? Engaging in an awkward conversation that neither of us wanted to be having? Forcing me to think about my loss in some random moment? Would it have been better if they'd said nothing at all? If I could write the instruction manual for these sorts of encounters, I'd say this: Be sensitive. Read the person in front of you. Look for an opening to be comforting beyond the pro forma "I'm sorry," and if the opening isn't offered, avoid the robotic response. Try to judge whether a condolence is welcome or wanted. And above all, be genuine. Don't feel obligated to say "I'm sorry" because society tells you that you should.

Since Heidi's passing I have been on a crusade to come up with something better, something more meaningful that I can say to someone who is grieving. I am still searching. I've often pondered what words would have comforted me. How do I balance the needs of others who are grieving with my own desire to be genuine? Unfortunately, I've had several friends lose someone, so I've had opportunities to test out new approaches. "That must be so hard" is one I draw upon. It connects on an emotional level with the person's pain. "I was saddened to hear the news" is another. These are just mine; you'll find your own.

At times of loss, most people want to be helpful; they want to bring comfort. Of course, there are some who prefer to not get involved, and that's okay. But most everybody else wants to be that helping hand, although so few really can be. Because of my own grief experience, and because I am an emotionally driven person, I've developed a desire to make myself available to those who are grieving, to offer something different from the usual conditioned response. Being able to connect with a person who's grieving removes the societal norm and allows me to go deeper.

Just recently, a friend of mine lost her husband suddenly and unexpectedly. I knew I needed to reach out to her and struggled with what to say. After taking some time thinking about my response, I came up with the following, which I sent to her in an email:

I know today is shock and awe. I know you'll be trying to figure out how to walk in this new world. I know how it feels the day after. I have been where you are about to go. Grief is a tough nut to handle, but it is possible to manage it, even though it may seem impossible right now. I was truly saddened to hear the news of your husband's passing. Please know that I am available to talk or to listen. I am here to support you should you want or need it. Feel free to call me anytime (you will not bother me).

Stay strong and intact.

Reaching out to people who are experiencing grief and loss, as I have, has become an important part of my healing process. I can never change what's happened, but by helping others and being genuine, I have found that I am helping myself, and, hopefully, them.

Dating

No advice section would be complete without addressing the 10,000 pound elephant—dating again. Less than four months after Heidi's passing, I found myself exploring thoughts of finding someone else. I am male, after all. It created conflict within me and filled me with guilt, but I couldn't help how I felt. I had been married to Heidi for over sixteen years; I didn't expect to be thinking about others so soon. It was easy to say there were no rules to follow and I had to listen to my heart, but thinking about looking for another felt deeply wrong. Regardless of the conversation I had within myself about timing and how I thought I should feel, I longed for companionship and intimacy once again. My longing wasn't an attempt to replace Heidi. It was recognition of my desire to have those feelings of affection, belonging, and togetherness back in my life. I missed being in a relationship.

Oddly, I was not the only one struggling with this idea of being alone. During a car ride, Madeline asked me if I planned to marry again. As we discussed it, she began to cry. She admitted she wanted me to meet someone, not just for my own happiness, but to have another woman in our lives. I realized that carrying the torch as the only female in our family was a heavy burden for a young teenager to shoulder.

Slowly I began to dip my feet into the dating pool. Dating in the twenty-first century is very different from what I remembered. Starting a conversation and meeting someone is as easy as a swipe to the right on your smartphone. I started out on several dating sites, but I didn't have the courage to be public; I wasn't ready for the accidental encounter with someone who might recognize me, and I wasn't ready to make a move with someone else. So I lurked in the shadows for a couple of months until my cover was blown by my inability to understand this techno-dating environment. By accident, I entered into a conversation with a female stranger, and I didn't blow up. I had taken my first step.

As I delved further and viewed pictures and read profiles, I found myself intrigued and excited about the prospect of participating in this modern dating phenomenon. Simultaneously, I was both intimidated and terrified of reentering the "game." I was torn between wanting to find someone and not knowing if I was ready to find someone. I boldly threw my line into the water and waited for a fish to bite.

It wasn't long until a woman took my bait. We texted for a little over a week and then made plans to meet. The idea of actually meeting someone filled me with anxiety. I hadn't dated, or even thought about dating, in over eighteen years. I also struggled with still feeling married and connected to Heidi, so this whole exercise felt a little bit like cheating. Of course, it wasn't, and I knew that, but it still felt odd and a little wrong.

I asked my prospective date where we should meet, as I had never thought about my city in the context of dating and had no idea what might be a quaint spot. She named a little wine bar. As I dressed for the evening, I hoped this bar might have something stronger than just wine. I was back in high school preparing for that awkward first date. I chose a button-down shirt and a nice pair of jeans. I decided to leave the sneakers home in favor of a pair of decent leather shoes. I would have put on some cologne, but I didn't have any. A final brush of my hair and a double check in the mirror, and I was off.

This evening was a very big deal. It was a major step in my ability to move forward and would be a determinant of my capacity to develop a relationship with someone new. This poor woman had no idea the role she was about to play. For her, it was another night of meeting some random guy she met on the internet; for me, it was a turning point in my life and a test run to determine my entire future, no pressure.

I was the first to arrive and had a few minutes to myself prior to receiving a text telling me she was parking. While waiting outside the bar, I exhaled deeply to control my blood pressure and walked through the greeting in my head: Should I shake her hand, hug her, or run away before she entered? What if she didn't look like her profile picture? What if we couldn't carry on a conversation? Should I have set up a "save me" phone call for a half hour in? My date walked around the corner, and all these thoughts and concerns disappeared. There she was, my emotional and social guinea pig, my first date in forever. We embraced and walked into the wine bar.

We sat down, ordered a glass of wine, and proceeded to talk. She looked like her online profile picture, and we were able to carry on a conversation without too many awkward moments of silence. These were good signs, but there were no sparks. We talked for close to two hours and then parted ways. After our date, I never saw or spoke to her again, and it didn't matter. She was so much more than a first date: she was a piece of my recovery. I had taken a huge step forward. The dating barrier had been breached, and I had survived.

As I continued down the path of dating, I realized that online dating was no place for those with weak character or self-esteem issues. I would swipe right, send out messages, make attempts at first contact, and many times I would hear crickets in return. The sounds of silence can have you questioning everything: Was I not witty enough, were my pictures not attractive enough, was my being a widower freaking women out? There were never messages sent back explaining why I wasn't contacted. On the other hand, I have received requests from older women, usually seven to ten years my senior. At my age, can older women still be called cougars? As much as I was flattered to be contacted, for now I was more interested in dating women closer to my age.

Throughout my lifetime, I have often looked back at a period in my history and wondered what it would be like to repeat that period with the life experiences and wisdom I've gathered during my adulthood. With dating, I've been given that chance. In my youth, at the peak of being single, I was awkward. I didn't have the confidence or the self-esteem to be successful. I was the shy kid in the corner who fumbled the pickup lines. Of course, I did meet Heidi, so I wasn't a complete disaster, but overall, I didn't date much.

Now, though I have been forced to reenter the dating world against my wishes, I can see it as an opportunity. I have the maturity and wisdom of decades of life experience in my tool box. There's no pressure to find the "right" person, and I don't need to start a family. Nevertheless, it has taken time to get comfortable with dating again. I've had to separate my relationship with Heidi and open myself up to a relationship with another, working through so much guilt and acceptance. I have given myself permission to pursue relationships with others without comparing. I won't be able to replace Heidi, so it's futile and self-sabotaging to try. I am looking for a new and different relationship, one that will bring me happiness and the companionship and intimacy I desire again. Perhaps she'll be a woman more comfortable in high heels than Converse sneakers; or be more into biking than baking, which would help my waistline dramatically. I am looking for someone to laugh with and who will love and enjoy my children as much as I do. I welcome the feeling of butterflies and the excitement of a new romance.

I will always love Heidi, but I believe it is possible to love again. If you are dealing with loss of a spouse, you will love again, too.

Parenting Your Children Through Grief

Behind the Behavior

When Jack was diagnosed with Type 1 diabetes at age four, Heidi and I learned to manage his rising and falling blood sugar. These fluctuations created mood swings we needed to identify and handle. Jack had always been a pretty even-keeled child. He followed the rules and rarely misbehaved. If Jack was acting out and being combative or argumentative, there was always a chance that it was because of low or high blood sugar. As we came to understand the mechanism at work, we developed an intervention strategy: prior to any disciplining, Heidi and I tested Jack's blood sugar to see if his numbers were out of range. If they were, we took a deep breath, treated the problem, and reminded ourselves that it was the disease acting out, not Jack. If he was within normal range, we disciplined him as usual.

Jack's diabetes was my training ground for handling the grief of three children. Like fluctuating blood sugar, grief created mood swings. It had the power to manipulate personalities in an instant. My challenge was to determine if the bad behavior was normal, and therefore needed to be dealt with in the usual way, or if it was caused by a moment of grief. I continually observed and evaluated my children. The last thing I wanted to do was punish them for grieving.

This came to light soon after Heidi's passing. The first night alone was not just difficult for me, it was difficult for the children as well. We needed each other, and we needed to come together as a family to remind ourselves that we still existed. We needed to be close. So we had a sleepover in Dad's room. Jack and Max climbed into my bed, and Madeline, age thirteen, settled in, close by, on a twin-size air mattress. Being together that night made things better, but poor little Max was struggling to find his place in this new world. He'd been quiet all day and lost. He continued to struggle throughout the night as well, his grief manifesting as physical symptoms. He couldn't sleep and complained of stomach aches and nausea. As the others slept, Max woke almost every hour. Three times he threw up from sadness. There was nothing I could do to comfort him, no medicine I could give him. I could only stay up with him and watch my youngest son age by the minute.

Max decided he needed to move into my bed to sleep long-term—new territory for me. After several weeks, I asked him when he might be ready to move back into his own bed. He'd answer that he wasn't ready, but he was getting closer. The night after that, I asked him why he liked my bed. I expected him to say something about security, emotional comfort, or anything sounding like a need for healing; what I got was "Your bed is more comfortable than my bed, and I like it better because you have a TV that I can watch until I fall asleep." That was not the emotionally distressed answer I was looking for; he was in his bed the next night, though he continued to bounce back and forth between my bed and his. After a while, my patience began to fracture; there were times when I didn't want to fall asleep to the TV or have the ceiling fan on. I wanted to sleep my way, in my own bed. I, too, was grieving and adjusting. Ultimately, Max made it back to sleeping in his room on a regular basis and rediscovered that his bed wasn't hard and uncomfortable like he thought.

I'm a patient person; it takes a lot to rile me up. But the ongoing drama of Max's bouncing between our beds was wearing me out and pushed me to the breaking point. However, in the long run, it offered me an opportunity to observe my child more closely and parent him on a deeper level. Our blow-up on October 21 reminded me that bad behavior, under our circumstances, might not be bad behavior at all.

Friendships

Friendships change after loss. Relationships remain the same, but being around others becomes different. I have seen this not only in my friendships, but in the friendships of my children as well.

Madeline has a friend Jenny, whom she has known since they were babies. As toddlers, they went to Mommy and Me events together, they went through preschool together, and now they attend high school together. For the last year and a half, Jenny and Madeline have carpooled to school, and on many occasions Madeline has come to me and discussed the interactions that take place during the morning car ride with Jenny and her mom. The bickering is nothing outside the norm between a teenage girl and her mother. The mother likes to dance or sing to the music on the radio, and the daughter is embarrassed by the spectacle her mother is creating. They argue and exchange a few heated words; the daughter reacts as if her mother has committed the most heinous of crimes, and, of course, her day is now ruined. The two love each other dearly, but a teenage girl finding her way and stretching her wings can make for a few tense moments.

Jenny and her mother would never willingly do anything to make Madeline feel uncomfortable or trigger thoughts of loss, but that's exactly what takes place. When Madeline witnesses these interactions, it reminds her of what a privilege it is to have a mother you can be this angry at or embarrassed by. It brings the void left by not having Heidi to interact with or guide Madeline through adolescence to the forefront of Madeline's awareness.

Madeline and Jenny have grown up together and have been close friends their entire lives, but Madeline lives in a different world now; she lives in a world where a car ride isn't just a car ride. Both Madeline and I live in a world where we can interact with our friends, but those interactions may trigger underlying responses that others are oblivious to. To maintain our friendships we have to manage our emotions. We have to be different, but look the same.

Therapy

In October 2015, I was referred to a nonprofit organization that provided group therapy, by age, to children who have suffered the loss of a parent. I took advantage of that referral and enrolled our family in the program. I had high hopes that being around other children who shared a common loss would help my kids with theirs. For the boys, the groups were helpful. Unfortunately, after three meetings it became clear that this group environment was not right for Madeline. As the boys and I continued, Madeline dropped out.

As 2016 was ending, Madeline was still having problems processing the death of her mother. She was unable to go to the cemetery without a tremendous fight. If the topic of Heidi's death came up, she became either quiet or argumentative. She couldn't bring herself to say, "when Mom died," "since Mom's death," or anything else that directly acknowledged Heidi's passing.

Over time, it became clear that, while it's hard enough to enter the teen years as a girl, it is exponentially harder to do so without the guidance and assistance of a mother. As a man, I suspected my lack of understanding about how it felt to be a teenage girl was an impediment to parenting her the way she needed. In an effort to be more motherly, my tendency was to overcompensate by nurturing her. I didn't want to force discomfort on her.

Yet, it was clear there were triggers in her life she needed to address and work through. I came to understand that Madeline needed a therapist who could help her address her issues one-on-one. When I informed Madeline that I had decided to send her for therapy, all hell broke loose. She was infuriated with me. She asked me multiple times if she had to go, and my answer was always the same: "Yes." She told me repeatedly that she didn't need a therapist, she was fine. The more argumentative she got the more convinced of her need I became.

I felt terrible forcing her to do something she clearly didn't want to do, but sometimes the best love is tough love. I knew she needed to address the feelings inside her and that it would be better done sooner rather than later.

I committed Madeline to four sessions with the therapist, one every week for a month. I felt it was important to get even the slightest buy-in from her, so I took a leap of faith and gave her some power in the decision. I told her she had to go four times; after that, it would be up to her whether to continue. I crossed my fingers that the therapist could break through to her in four sessions.

The night before her first appointment my hunch that she needed therapy was affirmed. That Sunday was a typical weekend day; Madeline was happy and joking around. Everything seemed normal. Just before heading out for dinner with Madeline and her brothers, I reminded her that I would be picking her up the next day at school and taking her to her first therapy appointment. In an instant, storm clouds rolled in, lightning bolts shot to the ground, and a tremendous roar of thunder filled the room. Hurricane Madeline had arrived and it was a category five. At the restaurant, Max and Jack complained that Madeline was kicking them under the table. Every sentence that came out of Madeline's mouth was a verbal jab; she was looking for a fight. If you said the sky was blue, she would disagree with you and call you a name for thinking that way. Every scowl and every aggressively toned statement began to peel off the layers of my patience. Even though I knew the meaning behind these outbursts, it was becoming more difficult by the minute to remain calm. It was a very long dinner.

When we arrived home, I sent her upstairs to her room. Of course, she refused to go. That was the small crack that destroyed the dam. Hurricane Gregg came in off the coast, and I let loose. I'm sure the entire neighborhood heard what came next.

Time gave us both a chance to breathe and calm down. I went into her room and sat on her bed. "This is going to be me talking and you listening," I told her. I proceeded to describe the obvious change in her when I'd mentioned the therapy session. I pointed out that she acted similarly whenever she had to face a moment of realization about Heidi's passing, like a trip to the cemetery or Mother's Day or an anniversary. I explained the importance of having a release for these emotions and that it was my hope that seeing the therapist would provide that release for her. I asked her to be honest and open and to give these sessions a chance. She responded by asking me again if she only had to go to four sessions and if I was going to honor my agreement not to force her beyond that time frame. I assured her that our deal was intact and that she was truly in charge after the initial commitment. Madeline's therapist had her work cut out for her.

One year out, Madeline was still seeing that therapist, and the change in her had been tremendous. She still could not go to the cemetery, but she could have honest talks about her emotions. She still could not say the words "Mom's death" or "Mom's passing," but she could have a conversation about it using facial and hand expressions as a substitute for the actual words. She started out kicking and screaming and cursing at me, but grew to look forward to talking and connecting with her female therapist.

Today, Madeline still sees a therapist occasionally. She can now go to the cemetery, but only by herself and not often. She still struggles with the actual words that pertain to Heidi's death. But she has come a very long way, and I am proud of her.

The resistance I received from Madeline when I first signed her up for therapy was a true test of my resolve. I could tell she was hurting, and the last thing I wanted to do was cause her more discomfort. Our fights were epic in scale, and it would have been much easier to back down and not push the situation. I trusted my instincts, held my ground, and stayed the course, and I'm glad I did. Without a release, Madeline's inability to process and contextualize her mother's death undoubtedly would have festered and worsened for years. Therapy was what she needed. Sometimes, the right decision is not the easy one.

Madeline's experience was the incentive I needed to continue to keep a close watch on my kids and look for signs of distress. I didn't have to wait long until another situation showed itself. Max remained in peer group therapy for over a year. Every time he went, he came face-to-face with his mother's passing; whether it was through art projects or discussions, her loss was always the topic. Unlike Madeline, Max could go to the cemetery and talk about Heidi without an outburst. It wasn't easy for him, and he became overwhelmed with sadness every time, but he could manage and get through it.

While Madeline's signs manifested outwardly in easily identified aggression toward me or her brothers, Max's distress was more internal and thus harder to see. On the surface, Max appeared to be doing very well; he was social and happy. Nothing seemed out of the ordinary. It took me almost three months to connect some tiny dots with him.

One day, Max woke up complaining of a headache and nausea. He said he felt like he was going to throw up and didn't want to go to school. I felt frustrated, because this was not the first time we were having this discussion, and while I didn't think he was sick, I also didn't want to force him to go to school feeling under the weather. Over several months it seemed like he had missed many days of school, always complaining of the same thing and always putting me in that same place of indecision. Previously, I let him stay home, and his symptoms never evolved; he always felt better by the afternoon. This time triggered me differently. I decided to look up his absenteeism online and see just how many days he had missed. He had missed some in January, some in February and now some in March; it was becoming a trend.

While investigating his absences, I was reminded of some conversations he and I had had about his third quarter grades. For some reason, that quarter, his grades were way below normal—not because he failed tests, but because he didn't turn in work. Homework assignments or projects were turned in late or not at all. When I confronted him, he blamed his teachers for not reminding him of the due dates, or being unclear with the directions, or not putting the right notes on the board. Everyone was to blame but himself. Max had always been a conscientious student; this behavior was outside the norm.

Max's physical ailments and lack of attention in school suddenly came into focus as related and not coincidental. Max had been out of peer counseling for just over three months, and it was during that period that these signs of distress began showing themselves. Parenting children through grief is like being a detective; you have to always be on the lookout for clues.

The next time Max stayed home from school I decided to put my theory to the test. I scheduled an appointment for him to see his pediatrician, and prior to our arrival, I called the doctor and shared my suspicions. I felt Max was internalizing grief and manifesting physical ailments as a result. Max's doctor gave him a full physical. Afterward, while Max sat in the waiting room, she agreed with my theory. Later that afternoon, I scheduled Max to see the same therapist who was helping Madeline.

The following week, Max went to therapy for the first time. I sat in on that session, and when the topic of his mom was brought up, Max tried to pivot. It was clear he was struggling with expressing emotions; he had a tough time defining how he felt. The therapist nudged him. As the session progressed I saw something that saddened and scared me and made me grateful I was there. Heidi's death and the emotions surrounding it were locked away deep within him. As the discussion continued, Max revealed how protected he had been keeping those feelings. He covered them with armor, kept them in a bunker, built a wall around the bunker, filled a moat around the wall, and then positioned guards around the moat. It was going to take tremendous effort to peel off the layers of his protection.

Max was in therapy for over six months, and it took great effort, but slowly, he started removing the layers around his guarded emotions.

With Max and Madeline both in therapy, my thoughts turned to Jack. I knew that Jack had to be affected by Heidi's death; we'd all been affected. Unlike his brother and sister, Jack showed no signs of distress; no excessive arguing and no abnormal physical ailments. Jack's surface seemed intact. Although there were no immediate fires to put out with him, I didn't want to be caught in a fire I couldn't see. With the others in therapy, I became concerned that Jack might have questioned why he hadn't been offered that option. I didn't want him feeling that I was favoring his brother and sister or that I was less sensitive to his needs. I asked him if he felt he should be seeing a therapist. He looked at me with shock on his face and exclaimed, "Hell no!" That was that. Knowing that Jack is okay for the moment is no guarantee that he will remain okay in the future. I continue to keep a close eye on him and monitor his behavior for any signs of distress. I have to believe that the time will come when he too will have to work through the rubble of Heidi's loss.

My kids are so different. They were raised by the same parents, grew up under the same roof, and shared the same experiences, but they are as individual as fingerprints. Their individuality has been one of my greatest joys to watch develop, and yet, under our circumstances, it has created one of my biggest challenges. Parenting them through grief has not been easy. It has required tremendous patience and a great understanding of who they are as people. I have had to be particularly sensitive toward the signs of grieving, which have shown themselves differently for each child. An outburst isn't necessarily an outburst anymore; an ailment isn't necessarily an ailment. Surface level difficulties may point to underlying grief, and I have to take the time to breathe, recognize, and evaluate. Children are not well-equipped to handle losses of great magnitude. As a parent, I've had to figure out what my kids need when they have no understanding of their behavior, and take action to support their grief process. Their emotional well-being depends on it. Therapy and peer counseling have been essential for my children's healing.

Working Out and Physical Activity

In addition to therapy, another aide in recovery is the gym. Jack has started to work out regularly. Max often accompanies me and shoots hoops on the basketball court, since he's too young to be in the weight room. Madeline has used the pool and the large array of treadmills and other cardio devices. The gym has become an opportunity for all of us to live more healthily, but also to work through frustrations and generate endorphins to help with grief. You can take out a lot on a treadmill. My children are fortunate to have gym access.

Visits to the Cemetery, Or Not

The kids have never come up to me and asked to go to the cemetery to see their mother. We have gone, but it has always been my decision as to when. I feel that it's important to get there at least a couple of times a year—mainly our anniversary, Mother's Day, and Heidi's birthday. But lately I've been asking myself why it's important. Why do I feel a need to go and stare at a headstone? It's not to speak to her, because I rarely say anything; it's not to remember our life together, because I think about that every day. For me, it's important to go so I don't lose touch. As my life moves forward, my memories become more distant. When I go to the cemetery, there is a physicality to being there. When I sit on the rocks above Heidi's grave, it's like I am recharging a battery that loses a little bit of power every day. People say that going to the cemetery to see the resting place of your loved one is paying your respects to them. I feel the meaning behind that statement. I feel that going to the gravesite, and having the kids go, honors the love we have for Heidi. Going there is a symbol that we haven't forgotten her.

For over a year Madeline refused to visit her mother's grave. I never would have probed further if it weren't for this book. I wanted to understand her resistance, so I asked her if she was willing to talk about it, in order to help other families. She agreed, as long as she could write her answers to my questions, rather than discussing them.

In her responses, she told me, "I wanted to think of the Mother's Days I spent with her, rather than just spending the day with her grave." She told me that going to the cemetery made her feel vulnerable and that she felt self-conscious about crying in front of other people.

I asked her if she regretted the times she hadn't gone with us, and she told me she didn't. "I don't have regrets," she wrote, "because even though I don't go to the cemetery I still think about her all the time in ways that I'm comfortable with. On her birthday, when you went to the cemetery and released balloons and I stayed home, I found some old photos of us with Mom. I later put them into frames and hung them around the house, so we can always look at the happy times, versus looking at a grave, which isn't a happy thing to me."

Madeline's responses made me realize how important it is to respect each of my children's ways of grieving. I asked Madeline if she had any advice for parents whose children might not want to visit the cemetery. She said, "I would tell them that you can deal with the situation and cope with grief in your own way because there is no right way, and not everyone is going to understand what you are going through."

And then she added, "But just make sure that you have someone that you can talk to because when you keep all of your emotions inside of you, they can build up and it's not that good."

I had felt disappointed that Madeline's therapy hadn't led her to want to visit the cemetery, but clearly, it had served her in other ways, and her visiting the cemetery was my wish, not hers. She understood how important it was to have someone to talk to, and she was reflective about the reasons she chose not to go with us. What's more, she had come up with her own observances for those occasions. How could I say her observances were any less respectful than what the boys and I did at the cemetery?

Acknowledgments

There are so many people without whom this book would not have been possible.

Christina Young: So many people told me I should compile my social media posts and put them into a book, and I thought they were all crazy. I trust your opinion because you're in the publishing business, and you're one of Heidi's close friends. I thought you would put all this craziness to bed. To my surprise, you agreed with the others and gave me the validation and the confidence to embark on my writing journey. You mentored me through that first year of posting and supported me in so many ways. This book never would have happened without you.

Kristin McGuffie: You were my first editor. You helped me create an outline and develop the structure of the book. You set the tone and taught me so much about how to project myself as a writer, not just the guy next door.

Gillian Culff: You were my second editor. Working with me for over a year, you were the backbone of this entire endeavor. We cried together, we laughed together, and we did great work together. Your support has been way beyond just a working relationship. I am proud to call you my friend.

Cynthia Manson: I went to a writers' conference looking for agency representation, and I was blessed to find you. You believed in my book from the moment we met. You connected to my story and worked so hard to find a publisher to take it on, even though my book is not the genre you represent. You supported me professionally and made me feel like I already had a best seller. You taught me so much about how publishing works.

Nancee Adams: You gave so much of your time as an editor, for free, to format the writing into a much more free-flowing narrative that enhances the book overall.

Judy, Madeline, Jack and Max: We all shared the same loss, but we experienced it so differently. Thank you for letting me share your journey publicly, sometimes voluntarily, and other times not so voluntarily. Your love and support helped carry me through this difficult time. This book is for all of us.

Ewa: You read the book early in our relationship and didn't run away. You accept and support this connection to my past without judgment or fear. You have shown me that love and happiness can be found again after tragedy. Thank you for making the choice to marry me and create a new and exciting future together.

Heidi: You passed away, but in doing so you passed on your voice and writing skills to me, something I never had before. I feel and have always felt that you were my co-author and we wrote this book together. Thank you for the time we had together and the beautiful family you left behind.